i'll tell you
one damn thing,
and that's
all i know!

Also by the author

CDs and other merchandise are available through www.jannarden.com.

Jann Arden Management,

P.O. Box 86034, 2106 - 33rd Ave. S.W., Calgary, AB T2T 6B7

Manager: Nikki Shibou

email: jannsfanns@jannarden.com

i'll tell you
one damn thing,
and that's
all i know!

jann arden

INSOMNIAC PRESS

Interior illustrations by Jann Arden
Author photo:
    Courtesy of Universal Music Canada; Photographer: Andrew MacNaughton; Hair: Stephanie J. Pogue, GoddessHair Inc.; Makeup: Melissa Gibson, MAC Cosmetics.

Library and Archives Canada Cataloguing in Publication

Arden, Jann
    I'll tell you one damn thing, and that's all I know / Jann Arden.

ISBN 1-894663-74-8

    1. Arden, Jann,—Diaries. 2. Singers—Canada—Biography.
I. Title.

ML420.A676A3 2004   782.42164'092   C2004-903942-3

The publisher gratefully acknowledges the support of the Canada Council, the Ontario Arts Council and the Department of Canadian Heritage through the Book Publishing Industry Development Program.

Printed and bound in Canada

Insomniac Press, 192 Spadina Avenue, Suite 403
Toronto, Ontario, Canada, M5T 2C2
www.insomniacpress.com

THE CANADA COUNCIL   LE CONSEIL DES ARTS
FOR THE ARTS   DU CANADA
SINCE 1957   DEPUIS 1957

ONTARIO ARTS COUNCIL
CONSEIL DES ARTS DE L'ONTARIO

To my mom and dad

—who, thank God, are still here
and busy spending my inheritance.
I sincerely hope that they are around
long enough to spend it all.

Introduction

As I read through my journals from the past couple of years, in preparation for publishing this book, I could not believe the contrast from one 24 hour period to the next. Some mornings I woke with more willpower and positive energy than anyone on the planet. Apparently as I slept, that glee, that pure joyfulness, would sneak out the back door. I would wake not knowing what I was doing and being unsure of how I felt, or what the point was. How could that happen overnight? My mother would always tell us kids, growing up, that as quickly as things could turn to crap, that's how quickly they could turn themselves around and be good again—very much like the way I have written these journals. One day great, fantastic! The next...well you'll get the picture.

The true journey of the human heart is indeed very difficult. I hope that as you read through these pages you'll recognize bits and pieces of yourself within them. We are so alike, and yes, so very different. But I think at the core of all humanity is the ability to love. No matter what language we speak or where we live in the world, the essence of ourselves is made of love. Love is really all I ever write about. Even tales about cleaning "Sweet Maries" from the cat litter, or watching my dad build a squirrel-proof bird feeder, it's all about love. I write about love because I think about love, at some level, every waking minute of the day. Love got me this far, I shall rely on it as I continue onward.

I have found, through the process of writing, virtually everything can be funny: death, fear, hatred...all pretty funny stuff when you really think about it. Writing about one's life has its advantages; you get to remember it all—or most of it anyway. It allows you to safely go back in time, where things cannot hurt you anymore. It is a wonderful exercise that I highly recommend. Make notes in this book; write all over the darn thing. You'll feel better.

I have often said to people that I am not a singer, but rather a writer of songs. Songwriting has always been how I define myself. I hear songs on each of these pages. If I could write two hour songs, believe me, I would. It is so much easier to sing things than to say them.

I write these journals like no one will read them. If I didn't, I wouldn't be able to jot down a single sentence. It would be impossible. I have learned a great deal from writing every day. I've learned that I am too hard on myself most of the time. Many of the people I know are as well. I think the key to a life well lived is to be gentle on your soul. This book is a way for me to do that; to forgive myself and get on with it all. Like my dad always says, "Don't be careful, be sorry" and "Don't bend over, bend down." Words to live by...

I know one damn thing...I just can't remember what it was.

jann

THE SPECIAL NITE

The special night
spent itself among the
flowers of darkness.
Only the wind whispered
" Come hither you
tired petal "
Bring yourself to my
caloused feet — lick
your wounds of
Imperfection.

— yeats

An Irregularity Of Being
May 15, 2002

No leaves on the trees. No green grass. Everything is late this year. Everything has been waiting for a clear opportunity. Every tulip. Every crocus. Every blade of grass, waiting for a ray of light. Shrodie is on my desk. He likes to sit on paper.

When you lose someone, you lose yourself. You want to go with them, even though it scares you half to death. When someone loses you, they pick up the phone a thousand times, start to dial and then hang up. They want what they cannot have. You have what you do not want, and yet do want with all your might, the paradox that breaks hearts every second of every waking day. It must be easier to go back, you say to yourself, "It must be...it has to be...easier...than...this." The perfect story that ends sadly, cannot be with, cannot be without. Typical of the journey we are on.

And then, they are with someone else. They move in, you move out. The calls are fewer and farther between. A voice picks up the phone...it is not theirs. Hanging up. Hung up. Hanging on. The thought does startle and sting. Lemon on a paper cut. A bug in your eye, peeling the lid back to find it, to get it out. A sliver under a thumbnail. Hot water burn...steam that cooks skin. A bloody nose. A broken arm. All of these things I would gladly rather have, than this. The without.

I send this to those who have lost. It's hard being a person. The sun will shine again. You have to wait for time to pass. It is the wisest of all things. Time. You must trust in that. Life is precious. You must never alter its state. It ruins us all to do so. It leaves holes that the wind blows through at night, stealing sleep, stealing peace, stealing hope. You will feel better. You will get better. Picture me and I shall picture you squinting into the sun. Everything will be fine.

jann

Waiting Out The Storm
May 16, 2002

I don't feel all that great. Just a bit queasy. Lofty. Moody. Trippy. Loopy. Slept for 10 hours, so that did me some good for sure...a little.... I think I've caused a major train wreck with making promises I couldn't possibly keep. I know I have. I got some tickets for a friend and said I would do something on a certain date for them, when I have actually got that entire block of dates already spoken for... I am a fucking idiot. Everything I say and do at this point, just makes it worse. I feel like I am in a Monty Python skit and I can't get out. I am an ass. Lock my doors, stay down. Wait for the storm to pass, killing all my livestock. I don't expect anyone to understand that.

More geese appear every day. Too bad all that shite isn't really a wonderful fertilizer. Life is like that. The cats are beating the crap out of each other. I yell, but nothing really happens. They stop for a second and then carry on their merry ways. Hairball in the bedroom. I thought I heard something in the middle of the night, but what it was is a mystery. No alarms were going off, so I assumed it was legal. That's all.

j

All Quiet
May 21, 2002

I have a moment to myself. When I travel, I just don't seem to get a chance to do anything other than travel. I don't like writing on the plane, too many other activities going on up there. I do have to mentally fly the plane the whole time and that takes energy!!

I am going out for a run. Outside is a far cry from the treadmill, which pulls one along quite merrily, I might add. You HAVE to keep going or perish underneath that blasted conveyer belt. I've been thrown off a number of times and Sweet Pea got a paw stuffed under there one time. It was horrible. Talk about burning hairs batman! She won't go near me now when I am on the thing.

I am still floating around somewhat. In my head and out of my head. I drift forward in time and then back through it, sifting things as it were. Sifting old things through my hands. I don't even really know why. I just am. I look at things and then set them back in their boxes. Back on their shelves. I open another box and stare and remember where and who I was. Not that it matters at all. I seem to know that. I still do it.

To be a person is a conflict, always. To be a spirit and a physical entity couldn't be a more difficult endeavour. You are always torn in two directions. You are never sure which is the right way. The right road. Faith is courage. Courage is faith. You will never be found, until you are completely lost.

j

The Beat Goes On
June 4, 2002

I think I wrote a journal some time last year. So much has been going on. Mom got her pacemaker; she is still in the hospital awaiting discharge. Apparently she picked up a bug and has an infection in the operation site. It's always something. She has been so blue. Anyway, she seems better today. I hope to God that she gets out this afternoon. I think what is going on with her now is so mental. She needs to be home in her space, in her chair, in her bed. Don't we all?

Dreamed I was a Hutterite. Lord.

j

Adrift
June 6, 2002

The sun is shining into the room. I can hear a cat purring like a mad old woman. The leaves are stretching themselves out of their little hoods. Finally. It is windier than a Carolina honey out there today (I don't know what that is). Still can't get over dreaming that I was a Hutterite. I know what I look like in polka dots now. It feels like I haven't worked in months. That's scary considering it's all I do.

j

Rainy Day Dreams
June 8, 2002

Ahh, the rain. Spitting like a teenage boy.

Water slips down the outside of my windows. It clings, in hopes of staying on. I like watching it roll down and join into itself at the bottom of the pane. I think glass is amazing. Who in the heck thought that up? How does one stumble upon something so glorious? "Look here Albert; if we burn the sand long enough, we can see right through it." Lord, purely amazing. To watch a glass-blower is pure romance. Perhaps I need to meet a glass-blower. Don't we all?

I am staying in all day. I am going to read fan mail. I am going to sit in the bath and stare up at the skylight and think of all the things I want to be. I am going to make grilled cheese sandwiches and tomato soup and popcorn and Crystal Light. I am going to order movies and watch soccer and cheer out loud here all by myself. I am going to sneeze and not cover my mouth. I am going to sit nude on the couch for at least 60 seconds and dry off without using a towel. I love doing that. I am going to chew all the pens in the house (if I can find one). I am going to feed the cats tuna out of a can. I am going to light candles and watch the sun go down. I am going to phone my mother (she was fast asleep an hour ago when I rang) and talk for half an hour. Why do people say fast asleep? Why fast? I am going to nap on and off and on and off again. I am going to phone my friend in New York and see what's new there. Poor old New York. Poor old world. Shrodie is watching the rain with me. His little head follows a single drop and then he loses it and starts on another. I am going to read until I cannot keep my eyes open anymore. I am going to pray until I fall asleep. Fast asleep.

jann

Sneakers And A Half
June 13, 2002

I hate feeling my heartbeat. You feel it when you're sad especially. I hate that. When you're happy, you don't have a heartbeat. You have a hum inside your chest that makes you want to laugh all the time.

I should get going, as I am picking the old girl up for a shopping trip. She thinks she can make it through half of Costco. What does one skip out on? So many horrid choices in life. Half of Costco. Unthinkable.

jann

Some Kind Of Wonderful
July 4, 2002

I have been away in a foreign land. It was nice to get away, but even nicer to get home. I want to be here to water plants and watch the cats walk around the yard. I want to putter and wash dishes and become a photographer. I want to take a course in glass-blowing and learn Spanish. I wish I could speak something other than bad English. Fat robins pull long worms out of the lawn; it's disgusting and charming all at once. I think I could eat a worm if I had to.

The house four doors down from me burned to the ground. Their propane tank blew up and burned their beautiful home down. What do you say to someone who has lost their lives? Sorry? You have this sick sense in your body of, "I am so fucking glad it isn't my house." My things. My clothes. My pictures. And then you want to cry for the poor people crying, standing in what's left of their driveway. It just makes you sick.

I look over at the black shell every morning and shake my head, saying what a shame. Hardly seems enough. It was a perfectly fine day. They went out to make some steaks or hot-dogs or hamburgers for their kids and two hours later, their house was gone. Fire. You can't win with fire.

ja

A Memory
July 5, 2002

Mom and I rollerbladed around the lake, well I did and she rode the bike. I thought she did great. It's been over a month now and all seems to be working as it should. I mean the heart and the wires and the batteries and such. We had fun looking at the new houses and yelling back and forth about

people's yards. It was one of those days that you store away in your heart. You say to yourself, remember this. This is a memory. Remember where the sun is. Remember her smile and her white hat tipped below one eye. Remember her little running shoes and the ring on her hand. Remember her laughing, trailing off behind you as the wind races through your sleeves and up your red shorts from Costco. It was a good day.

Dad came over later in the afternoon and fixed the holes in my dinghy. He brought over a repair kit and showed me how to fix a leak (I could have used this information in my teens). He looks so young. He said he saw a picture of Jack Nicklaus in the newspaper and he thought it was him. It could have been. That is exactly what Dad looks like. Only he doesn't golf as well.

ja

The Music Man
July 6, 2002

Timothy White died yesterday. He was a friend of mine. He had been the Editor-in-Chief of *Billboard Magazine* since 1991. He had a heart attack at 50 years old. What a shame, what a crying shame. He has two children. I think they are about 7 or 8 years old. You wonder what must go through a person's mind as they lay there staring at the ceiling in their office. All I know is that man enjoyed his life.

He was a music journalist for half of it. Not only was he a music journalist, but indeed, the nation's biggest and smartest music junky. He wrote an article about my *Living Under June* album in 1994, that changed its course completely. It was one of his "Music To My Ears" columns. Here I was, reading about my record in *Billboard Magazine* and it was wonderful. Timothy made me feel, after so many years of trying, like I had reached a pinnacle, a peak, a precipice of accomplishment; not only as a singer, but as a songwriter. It changed me. It changed how I felt about what I was doing. At that point in time I didn't even have a US release and after the article came out, we had calls come in from so many other labels. It was one of the most influential things that had ever been written about me. Everything after that was different. I was someone now. I had never been someone before. It felt amazing. I am forever in Timothy White's debt. I honestly believe he was single-handedly responsible for the success of *Living Under June* everywhere around this world.

Thank you sweet Timothy for being the music man. For being the ears that the world will so profoundly miss. For being the integrity that built the country's premiere music magazine into what it has become and will hopefully continue to be. Thank you for being the bar unto which all things musical were measured and compared. You knew what was good long before anyone else would ever admit to it. You didn't need to wait and see what other people thought. You knew what you liked and appreciated, even what you didn't always get. You were fair.

You always told me to "drop by" the office any time I was in New York. You will never know, or perhaps you do know, how much that meant to me. A country girl from rural Alberta invited to "drop by" the *Billboard* offices!!!!! And you meant it. That was the thing with you. It was a thrill that hung about on my spine for days on end.

I ate across from you at a picnic of some kind once, and you had two raviolis on your plate. You said that people didn't need so much food, that it wasn't good for them. I never forgot it. I met your children and your wife and I remember thinking how great your life was and how great your family was and I was proud to know you and proud that you knew me by name. I guess 50ty wonderful years is enough. It was for you, but not for us.

Say hello to Janis and Waylon and Ella and Karen and Jimi will ya? God bless you and keep you for all eternity.

jann

Steaming
July 11, 2002

I have been soaring across the land again. Back and forth, up and down, sideways, byways, under and over.

My mother, whom I talked with yesterday, told me Dad was at the house shampooing all my rugs. Who does that? What parent does that? I am picturing my father with my mother's prized rug shampooer, scaling up the stairs, steaming all the while. Steaming out of his mind and steaming the actual rugs. They do so much for me. I think I need to do something for them, although I have never learned how to use the shampooer. I asked my mother what she wanted for her birthday a few years back and that shampooer was the only thing she wanted. She said it was the best birthday she ever had. Now if it were my birthday, I would have wanted someone who came with the thing to work it...(I would feed them of course).

j

Wish Filled Thinking
July 14, 2002

When you wish wellness on others, you wish it too, for yourself. It is a universal blessing. It is a universal gift. What you wish for others, you wish for yourself. You will be what you want others to be. You become your thoughts.

jann

300 Days
July 17, 2002

I am homesick. I have been out here for almost three weeks. I want to go home. My life is very glamourous; I travel 300 days a year. I love it. I hate it. It is always a conflict for me. I am never comfortable, no matter where I am. I am too busy to realize how great my life is. I think about that all the time. I am not looking into my own God. I am waiting for this external thing to pick me up and save me. There is no external thing. It is internal. I know it is. Other than that, I am fine. Really.

Today is a new beginning to an old ending. Or is it a new ending to a new beginning? I feel like starting over. From scratch. From the word go. The nice thing is, you can do that every day.

j

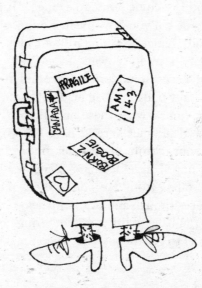

Holiday Home
July 24, 2002

I have been home for 3 glorious days. When I arrived, I had my friends from Edmonton sitting in my driveway in their motorhome with dinner ready for me. My friend Stephanie came out an hour later with bottles of spirits and bread and her famous parsley salad. They were apparently going to do something like this for me on my 40th birthday, but it just didn't pan out. I was in Newfoundland—I miss that place... So there we were, celebrating that milestone yet one more time. Hurray. It was one of those days you make note of. You store every ray of light. You put it away, a day like that, and you save it for your deathbed. As Sean Cullen would say, "Never get into your deathbed."

We all sat on the deck and watched the sun slip into the lake as the kids flew around on skateboards. The garden is 8 feet high and climbing. I don't know what to make of it. 3 weeks away and I've come home to a jungle. It just looks marvellous. I cannot tell you how much I enjoy watching everything grow and change and mutate and blossom. Having children must be a mind blower. I can't imagine. I figure with all the advances in modern science, I'll be able to have a child outside of my body in a bag made of Saran wrap well into my 120s. Who knows what these nutballs are thinking up.

I have missed summer here. I have been reading about it and hearing about it from my mother, but as for seeing it for myself, I have not. I have been in a plane or a bus or a cab or a hotel room, rolling from one side of the bed to the other. I love seeing places though and by George, you have to move to get to them. You have to lift your lumbering body up from its couch and travel to get them. That's what makes life so interesting. I know the cliché about life not being a destination, but rather a journey, and it is true. I can vouch for that. To look down at a cloud...who would have ever thought?

ja

Cosmic Experience
July 27, 2002

Had a few days of looking out at the lake and thinking about the world spinning around in space. How does the water stay so still? How does the sun not hurl us off into nothingness? How do we live? How can air be so big and so important? How can we see and hear and know things? It has been a week of this it seems. I enjoy the way the cosmos fucks with my head and my spirit. If God is indeed in me, that would explain the weight.

I talked to Diana Krall today. She sounded so clear and near, but she was in Korea of all places. That girl works harder than anyone I know. She goes and goes and lights up the world on her way. She's done so well and is still so grounded and solid. I am jealous of where she is and what she has done. I should've taken piano lessons I guess. I took trumpet lessons in Junior High...look where that got me. Anyhow, safe travels D. Holy flier miles is all I can say.

I cannot believe I am a person most days. I feel like a plastic bag hanging from a barbed wire fence. Oh well, beats being nothing at all.

j

How Dry
July 30, 2002

I just did an hour of cardio. I am going to go upstairs and eat the table.

j

A Couple Of Kids

August 13, 2002

I am in LA to mix the symphony record with my old pal Eddie Cherney. He is a master of sound and texture. We actually got in yesterday, Russell and me. We ended up going to Disneyland to hang out for the afternoon, as we were not supposed to start mixing until today. We rented a Mustang convertible and headed off on the 405. Sweet Mother of God, I forgot what it was like to drive here. You gotta put your foot down and leave it down.

It was really quite funny, the two of us wandering around like a couple of kids, eating ice cream and waiting with baited breath to board the rides with the rest of the throngs. We laughed all day long at ourselves, big toothy grins that harkened back to being 10 years old. I remember Pirates of the Caribbean like it was yesterday (I think I was in Disneyland 25 years ago...). Anyway, the ride still holds you captive with the fireballs blasting from pirate ship to pirate ship, the one-eyed men in striped shirts hoisting a beer to their lips—so lifelike indeed. The chests filled with silver and gold and crown jewels spilling out into the fiery night. We were so quiet going through those wonderfully crafted caves; we just kept nudging each other as if to say, "Gee whiz, cool hey??"

We went on Space Mountain and I swear it was the scariest 98 seconds of recent memory. I never stopped screaming; neither did Russ. We have a picture he bought for $12.95 that captures our open mouths and clenched hands as we rounded a tight corner. It is the funniest picture. We look happy though and that is what I will remember. We ate BBQ chicken and then drove home with the top down. We must have ridden every ride in the joint. 5 hours of buzzing about like we were on some kind of drug. And we were; it was called imagination.

I think the record is going to be really wonderful. It's so full of whimsy and colour and lightness—whatever that may mean. I remember the night well. It was the second Vancouver show that we are concentrating on recording, so listen for yourself (if you were at that particular show).

j

The Voice
August 16, 2002

We are born with a voice in our heads. It's with us in the womb, comforting and directing and guiding and soothing. Why it changes at some point is anyone's guess. It just does. Either our parents bend the voice trying to control us, or our friends change the voice, or our egos change the voice. Something does. Something changes how we talk to ourselves. We start out knowing that we can win and end up hoping we will fail. The voice tells us that we cannot win. The voice says, "How dare you even think you could be anything other than what you already are?" We get programmed to think we are not able or capable or worthy. Perhaps the human condition is one that involves constant criticism. We are harder on ourselves than we would ever be on any of our friends. We would never talk about our friends the way our "voice" talks about us.

You have to keep going, even when you don't have a clue where you are going. You are fine the way you are, or are you? You know when you need to change. It's just hard taking the first step. You have to tell your feet to move. I just want to live. I'll take every blow and I will keep trying to find the girl that walks the hallways of my middle-aged body.

jann

LA Times

August 18, 2002

I am still in LA. I went to a little club with Russell tonight called the Mint. Emm Gryner was playing on the bill along with Leona Neass. Emm was fantastic. She's one of the good ones. Pretty, compact, electric and effortless. Why she is unsigned is so beyond me, I don't know... She has a song called "Beautiful Things" that is just amazing. It is simply wonderful songwriting.

In other news...my voice was kinder today. I needed the break from the other one; that other voice can be withering. It leaves you thirsty. But today for some reason, it was breezy and sweet like a kiss. You just never know what it's going to say at any given time. I'll get it right one of these sunny long days. I do wonder why though. I would never want to be young again. I am content just to remember the carelessness. It was something, wasn't it?

I need to go to bed. I am being lofty and sober and I am going to shut up. The air conditioner in here is so loud that I can't hear my voice at all... Good.

ja

A Shadow
August 23, 2002

My mother is doing fucking great! She will outlive us all. My dad said that when she dies, he'll have to kill her. Things are back to normal.

jann

There Are Times
August 26, 2002

There are times when I feel like killing the people I love most. There, that's a good way to start the day off. I can't imagine there being anything more important than communicating with another person—and I mean communicating effectively. Communicating with empathy and concern and sincerity. Why else would there be more than one of everything? Why would there be a point to having children or making movies or writing books? It's about communicating some kind of ancient cry that we are indeed here and are going to be here for infinity. That we are not alone, although we are...very alone...alone because we are the same person essentially. WE are stuck together. I can tell that I am in a strange state because I have not the slightest inkling what I mean. No matter.

I read fan mail for about 6 hours. I really do enjoy reading all the random thoughts thrown my direction. It's like I am stealing something and I don't know what. I suppose we all steal from each other. We steal a wee bit of happiness from passersby; it somehow keeps us going from moment to moment. I should quit now. I just read this and I am being weird.

Shrodie is outside, hunting again no doubt. I should go and find him before he drags home a neighbour.

j

Headlines
September 3, 2002

Sometimes it's hard just knowing when to start, or stop—it depends what you're doing. Today it was hard to start anything: my brain, my legs, my arms, my mouth. I just wanted to lie in my cool bedroom—wind blowing the curtains up, cats all sound asleep, geese honking from somewhere out on the water—and not move. I know I lay there for a while not thinking a single thing. It felt like a relief of sorts, just to breathe in and out...

I haven't been reading the paper. I used to everyday and now I seldom do. Even the *New York Times* is getting to me, I fear. Even the damn book reviews... It seems that journalists are determined to fuck up my day by telling me what's going on out there. Not their fault I know, but Jesus H. God, could we put the sports on the first page at least? Could we put a scratch and sniff dog bum???? I mean, anything would be better than a politician or a blown-up car or a tornado or a flood washing some poor bastard out to sea. Could we put some grade 3 drawings of cows? Could we put Sonny and Cher on the cover every now and again and again...? Okay, forget that... maybe just Sonny.

j

Freckles
September 17, 2002

You go away for two weeks and upon returning, find that fall has moved in next door. What a marvel really. I was at a red light yesterday and found myself surrounded by blowing leaves. It was incredible. They danced around my head and played the loveliest song. It was a whisper that warned of snow and ice and frozen breath. I am looking forward to it all. I can start wearing my puffy coats and vests, my big blue boots and my wool hat with the word "Canada" scrolled around its brim. I am not really a summer person at all. I am winter and fall and yellow leaves and twigs and brown grass. It suits me fine; I can truly tell you that. I would rather be chilly than warm. I would rather see my breath than NOT see it. I just would. I am glad to be home, among my things and my pictures. I feel comforted by this place and that's all a person could ask for in a home. I had one less freckle when I awoke this morning...everything fades.

ja

News From The Wood
September 18, 2002

I let Shrodie out. He sits by the door and guilts me into opening it. I always do. I would like to put a camera on his little head and watch where he goes sometimes. God only knows. I am quite sure, at this point, that he does indeed have a whole other family going on and has for quite sometime. They most certainly do not get their food from Costco, but rather some upscale fishmonger... What else could have lured him away from the luxury around here? Okay, so the cat food I serve smells like shit, but isn't that the point? It's just cutting to the chase if you're asking me. I have to clean those boxes of "Sweet Maries" out today. I usually do it everyday, but yesterday was a busy one, so I left the little gems in there to sweat it out.

I learned a thing or two in Brownies, you know. I remember eating brownies in Brownies and I am not kidding. All we did was have bake sales. What's up with that? I don't recall having a "bake sale" badge. My dreams of being a Girl Guide were never realized. Oh well. I still have my health.

My nephews are 3 years old. Their birthday was on the 11th. I think they got tricycles. Can you even believe that? Where the heck does the time go...? On my ass, that's where.

j

Dinner Plans

September 20, 2002

It rained here last night, either that or somebody pissed all over my yard. I have to keep my eye on that neighbour of mine... I turned my furnace on the other night. I hated to do it, but the icicles on the cat's asses looked uncomfortable. They could poke an eye out with one of those things. Shrodie is out again. He is drinking again, I fear. Won't look me in the eye and his gums stink. I have beer missing. What can you do? I travel so much that they have made lives for themselves that don't include me.

My parents come home from Spokane today. My mother said the meals were huge. "Dad and I have been trying to split every meal," she said. They have been doing that at home for 44 years, so I don't see what the big difference is. My mother has ONE piece of toast every morning and a HALF a cup of coffee. That is it. She then proceeds to swallow 67 various vitamins. My dad has oatmeal; it's supposed to be good for high blood pressure. He quit taking his pills, as they made him feel worse than shit he said. Now, that's bad.

My parents are homeopathic as well as "they say" medical practitioners, "Well, they say if you take cod liver oil every day, your elbows won't ache." Really? I actually started taking it for a sore elbow (can you even believe it?) a few years ago and it went away—the ache that is, not the elbow (although that would not have surprised me one little bit). I know. I know...

Anyhow, I gotta go. I have read the *Oprah* magazine in my bathroom so many times that I dream about it.

j

A Prayer For Danielle
September 21, 2002

Light is all you are. A blinding white that cleans us all and
keeps the night at bay. May your restlessness be smothered in
the deepest of sleeps. Heavy and weighted down will you be
with peace and quiet. Your breath effortless. Your breath
effortless. Your heart forgiving and all merciful.

May you find ease in every moment and clarity in your
every thought. May pain be shattered and liquid and poured
down at your feet. May fear be washed from all your days. May

it be kept far from your house at night, locked away by hope and triumph. May you never feel alone, for you are never alone.

Love is perched at the foot of your bed while you sleep and upon your heart when you awake. Love surrounds and abounds and soars and saturates and lives in your life. Love is everywhere. You are the miracle we all pray for. You are the beacon we are running towards.

Give me your rocks, your albatross, your worries and I will share them with you. I will carry you as far as my own legs will take us both. I know you would carry me. We are facing the same direction. No going back, for it would serve no purpose, no gain, no worth. Until I drop and we both fall, so shall we go. For friendship is the house in which we find shelter from all things hard and sad. Be easy with yourself. Be kind to your soul. Let go. Let go. Let go.

You are beauty so astounding and so strong and blissful. There are no words to compare you to anything else in the heavens. Cry for the world you do and we are bathed in your struggle to find serenity. We cannot know why. We simply go on.

Thank you Danielle, for being the miracle we all pray for. God has found his truest soldier and how you boldly march for we who do not always believe.

j

Room With A View
September 24, 2002

It is pitch black outside. I wonder what "pitch" means when one is talking about black? And what is "ass over tea kettle"? Some moving vines just scared the living crap out of me. Fuck...there could be someone looking in at me right now and I wouldn't know, because when you turn on a light on the inside, it erases the light on the outside. I hate that about the night. I have to admit, that on a few occasions, mainly from the boredom of a hotel room, I have watched people go about their lives. I have sat in a chair and watched them talk on phones, or change channels, or eat, or just walk about.

I once saw a guy do a little ditty to himself while seemingly looking back at me. It was one of those moments when you scream silently and then run and get your manager so she can check it out too. At one point in the evening, we had the entire band at this little window in one of the hotel rooms, laughing to the point where we thought we'd faint. Imagine our giant heads straining to catch a glimpse of a penis, for God's sake. Talk about losers. It was a fun night, now that I think about it again. To this day, we call him Naked Man. Apparently the hotel where I stay in Toronto got a lot of complaints...about him.

j

Nutbar Recipe
September 26, 2002

I called home, but got the machine. It's my mother's 6-year-old message that makes my heart melt down my arms every time I hear it. She is so sweet and nice. Both my parents are nice people. I didn't always think that my dad was nice, but in hindsight, he was just that. He was also very fair, stern, but fair. When I think of what I might have gotten myself into had I not been fearful of him!!! Parenting is a nightmare I am sure.

Martha Stewart is on the TV behind me, on the Food Network. What a nutbar (she has a recipe for a nutbar I am sure).

ja

Soul Food
October 1, 2002

I miss my grandmother. I hope she is missing me too.

j

Ticklish
October 2, 2002

It would be pleasing if one could tickle one's self, no? Just for a lift and a giggle to get your day up and running. I am very, extremely, horribly ticklish. I never used to be. I don't think I was anyway. I don't remember if I was. I guess I already said that.

My older brother used to sit on me and fart. I don't know what was worse: the fact that he was farting on me, or that he was tickling me at the same time. It was awful, funny, but awful. I would laugh hysterically the whole time it was happening, so he thought it was all okay. He never seemed to have an ease of spirit. He always seemed weighted down. All these years later, he still is. I wish I could help him, but I can't.

ja

Unsure
October 5, 2002

Well, it's been a very strange day indeed, as far as the weather goes. It was snowing in white solid sheets at 9 a.m. this morning—I guess you knew it was morning as I had already mentioned that it was 9 a.m. Shall we carry on? Somebody picked up the world and gave her a big ol' shake. The flakes were the biggest I've seen since I was 9 years old. They floated down to the grass like a beautifully choreographed ballet, in and out of each other like a million tiny kisses. I loved watching it. The cats loved watching it. We sat at the kitchen table and wondered if we would ever see anything so pretty ever again. It's all gone now, not a single memory of it lies anywhere. Not one single flake. I guess it was supposed to be rain.

It was cold today. I went and saw my nephews for an hour or so and our walk was cut short by our frozen breath hanging in the air. They didn't care for it all that much. They are the cutest little pods. They never stop moving. Do you think that's the trick? To NOT ever stop moving?? I thought it was to "stop" moving...I am so confused.

My mom and dad were in fine form. They have been reading an advance copy of the book (my book). It makes me nervous to think of them reading about a botched hand job. Oh well, nothing like the present moment. May as well just get this stuff out of the way before Christmas comes. My dad said he was really enjoying it. My mom said that reading about Gram made her blue all over again. It made me blue writing it all down. Anyway, it seems weird that I even have a book. It's not really a book at all, though...it's a wander jot. Yeah, that's what it is.

Sweet Pea is in my computer case. I should zip it up and wing it around...no I'd better not. I think she's getting better at English. I swear to God she says, "What, what." I shouldn't drink this early...

jann

Rehearsals
October 9, 2002

I have been in rehearsals here in Vancouver for the big Cancer fundraiser tomorrow. Everybody is singing with everybody. I am doing a Spice Girls song with Bryan (God help me). Well, not a Spice Girls song, but one of his songs that a Spice Girl sang. Sarah is singing with me, I am singing with her, Chantal is singing with me, I am singing with her, Ed from BNL is singing with me and so on... We practised the finale today—it's a secret. I will tell you that it's not "We are the World," or even worse would be Canada's version on the same theme, "Tears Are Not Enough" (that was Ed's idea). At least Bryan could have sung his part, I could have done Luba's part and BNL could have easily stepped in for the Glass Tiger people. Chantal could do everybody else's parts—she's young and has more energy than the rest of us. Oh well, maybe next year.

Yesterday we rehearsed at Sarah and Ash's place. It's like an oasis where they are, the enchanted forest, Avalon. I was blindfolded and spun around, so I don't have a fucking clue where they live—somewhere here in BC. I would suppose.

The hotel I am in is nice. I was hoping to stay where the Queen just stayed, maybe run around her room with an empty jar and try and capture a royal windy pop...if you know what I mean. No luck. I'll just have to imagine that a royal fart would have hints of caviar and champagne. Mine are kind of like Oh! Henry and Chicken McNuggets (the French spell things funny, don't you think?).

I had the weirdest dreams last night. I don't know what they were, but they were terrible whatever the case may be. I dreamt I was sleeping. What's that all about? How can you dream that you're sleeping? And in my sleeping dream, I was dreaming. Very screwy if you ask me.

ja

New Friends

October 16, 2002

The world has been whirling around my legs for a week. I have not stopped, although being home has at least been a bit of a pause these past three days. I don't know how else to live. I am so used to going, going, going. I get home and want to go. I go and want desperately to come home. I am somewhat of a Nomad (or is it Nimrod?). What is a Nimrod? I hope it has nothing to do with a penis.

The concert in Vancouver was a feast for the head and heart. I can't actually remember a lot of it. I just remember the strains of beautifully sad sounds coming out of Sarah's mouth and twisting up into the rafters. She has doves whooshing around her hair, I swear. BNL were pinning us all back into our seats with laughter and throwing us about with their energy. They do so many things well. They are the nicest people you could ever meet. I feel like I have new friends. Maybe I can stay at their houses and eat meals with them when I am on the lamb (or I could just eat lamb). I watched *Silence of the Lambs* yesterday. Spooky shit. Makes you wanna lose weight... When Jodie Foster said, "Yes, she was a big girl" to the murderer, I laughed my arse off and I don't even know why.

Bryan really should eat meat. My God that guy has had a few hits over the years. When he gets playing them one after the other after the other, your jaw drops a bit more every time. I enjoyed humping his leg I must say...long, long story. He wanted me to act like a crazed fan, so, by George, I did. Chantal did a terrific job setting up the night. It is a hard slot to fill and she did it with flying colours.

I wish I had some dirt on everybody, but it was all quite civilized. No fights. No drunken mishaps. No nothing, just a lot of fine music and a lot of working together to make the whole thing come off without a hitch. I was just glad to be there. Did Vicki G the next day and I swear I was still half asleep. I think I fed a monkey. I hadn't had my decaf yet, so I could have been feeding Vicki...that didn't sound right either did it?

I feel like I have been doing laundry for two months (well you have you ass). I folded the last pile last night and then watched Shrodie drill a hole into it all and go to sleep. I didn't have the heart or the energy to move him. Everything I own has a fur collar. Very "in" they tell me. Very Versace (is that woman a nutbar or what?). Every time I try on anything Versace, I somehow manage to look like a sausage link. Is that good? That can't be good.

Well, I am going to make a latte and sit and watch the geese for a wee bit. 300 of them descended on the lake the other night while I had dinner with friends. It was a marvel. My friend's two year old didn't say a word for at least 2 minutes, watching them all come down and land on the water. They were resting apparently. Why the silly buggers were heading north is anybody's guess. Probably a man in the lead... I would love to fly like that for a day. Just one day to flit around and shit on some poor unsuspecting man with a brief-case...or just maybe someone I know, for a laugh—like Russ. Kidding buddy. I am doing nothing today. I think I'll do even less than that, come to think of it.

j

Jealousy
October 20, 2002

Jealousy is sinfully sweet. We cannot seem to get enough of it. I think when you have been bitten once, jealousy moves in for the kill. What I mean by that, is when you have been betrayed somehow, physically or mentally, when you lose trust in someone, jealousy moves in permanently. It brings its toothbrush and takes the spare room. You hear it in there at night watching Leno. "Need anything before I go to sleep?" it calls. "One last reminder of how weak you are???" I hate the feeling of helplessness, the feeling of being jealous.

You have to believe in yourself. Bit by bit, you have to believe in your goodness and your grace. You have to convince yourself of your worth, which is so great, it is not countable. You have to let go of fears and worries and live a freer life. You have to get over being afraid of being alone. We are all alone; to find comfort in that will make you live longer. It's not that we don't WANT each other, but do we have to NEED each other so much? I think that is where the haze sets in. Needing makes the boat rock.

You WANT the right person; you NEED the wrong person. You want someone you can be alone with. Being alone together, that is the tricky part. That would be perfect really. There is an old sock for every old shoe. I believe that. If you don't trust someone, there is no point in being with them. If you are tied to someone else as you climb up a mountain, don't you have to trust them completely?? Why would you even bother climbing up in the first place if you didn't? You have to completely trust that they will not let you fall, period. See what I mean? Trust. It's a hard thing to win back once it's spoiled. Not trusting is mixed in with jealousy and fear, so make sure you have it all sorted out before you say the wrong thing.

j

Have To Run

October 24, 2002

It is often hard to find the time to just sit with yourself. The race for the finish line, that moves ever forward, seems pointless, yet we continue to run until we fold our legs into bed at night. We crumple ourselves into a ball and hope that the next day is long enough to finally get everything done. We will NEVER get everything done. You must choose your battles and chip away at them for a lifetime. That is the road. That is the simple task. Plod. Plod. At least when you are plodding along, you can see both sides of the ditch and I will tell you, many treasures lie there waiting to be picked up and carried away.

Why we want the "blur" is beyond me. Perhaps it's the wind in your mouth that forces the air into your lungs. For a meagre moment, you don't have to breathe for yourself. I do want that, I just can't sustain it for long. My hair ends up too fucked up and I pull my eyebrows so closely together, that there is only one of them holding my face upright. Attractive, I think not. I want to wander through my life; I don't want to run. It's not a marathon; it's a nature walk.

I love what I do, but it scares me half to death most days. I am afraid people will find out how lost I am. That I really do not know what I am doing, that I just wing it (I do wing it). I think anyone that says that they know what they are doing, is essentially dangerous. They don't ever know what they are doing. They are playing a wicked game of chicken with themselves. I would rather be with someone who thinks they know; at least they are willing to accept suggestions. This whole thing, life, is a group effort. When somebody says they "know," they, more often than not, screw the rest of us with a large dose of blinding pride. I have to get plodding here pretty quickly...

I have been running and running and running. Sometimes I think if I stop, I'll lose everything and have to go back to the beginning, when really, going back to the beginning every morning is exactly what I want to do. I want to be able to create a new person without a history, without a mistake made, without a jagged memory that catches the corners of your eyes and makes a tear ruin your makeup. I want to fly into the world today, like I have never seen it before and it has never seen me. That is the gift of forgetfulness. I don't want to remember every single thing I have ever done. I want to surrender to new things, new days, new experiences. I want to know what I know and actually use the damn stuff.

We have so much information that we never ever use. We know what we need to do, but we just sweep it under the rug with our integrity and our dignity and our mercy and our grace and our humour and our forgiveness. We have so many tools that we never use. The ego is so much louder than the spirit; it can eclipse the soul's haunting whisper. That is why you have to sit still, be quiet and listen for that little voice. It's polite and patient and it wants you to hear it. You have to talk back to it and acknowledge that it's getting through. That's not much to ask. I know we need to ask the right questions of ourselves. I am just learning that now.

j

Insider
November 6, 2002

I am in New York at present, overwhelmed with every light bulb blinking on and off forever and a day. I am overwhelmed with the food steaming on every street corner and taxicabs riding their horns like they may get a food reward. Like rats in a box in the middle of some lab somewhere, they drive around blindly looking for some worn out sap to flag them down. The smart ones are down underneath it all, clamouring around in a tin subway car, reading their books and waiting to take their shoes off.

Had dinner at Lupa the other night...my favourite! Went to some wacky party at Hilary Swank's house afterwards. Her husband, Chad, had a few people over after the play (he was the lead, opposite my friend Sherri). Anyhow, it was a gigantic mansion that was beyond my idea of a big gigantic mansion. The Lowe/Swanks are just now moving in. They tell me (the insiders) that this was once Gwyneth's joint...who really knows. There was a fireplace in every room—I kid you not! I felt like a voyeur. I felt like I was breaking into someone's heart. The point being, that I felt weird being there and I don't even know why.

I went to the bathroom at one point and low and behold, not a single square of toilet paper. I managed to pinch my knees together and crawl over to a pack of "Jerry cloths," (you know the disposable throw away dish rags???) I took one out, wiped myself up and flushed it down the drain. I prayed that it wouldn't clog the toilet for the next guest. Can you imagine? I plugged Chad and Hilary's toilet before they could!? Sheesh.

ja

Out This Window
November 12, 2002

    I have been sleeping for two days. My body went that's it, lie down and DO NOT get up. I have done all my laundry; it is waiting now for me to put it away. I have so many bras. I have to stop buying them for a while. I cannot fit them all into the bra drawer. I need to start another drawer perhaps (can one take bras to the Goodwill??). Who in the world would want a used bra? I don't know if I would want to go there.

    I had such a great time in New York. It is the most interesting city I have ever been in. It's so busy and full of sounds and shouting and horns and people and motion and cars and taxis. It does not stop. There is never a lull. You'd think that at 5 a.m. in Times Square there would be some kind of stillness. There is not, nor will there ever be.

    I hope Hilary's toilet is working...

ja

Back For More
November 13, 2002

I like Calgary. It's slow and lazy for the most part. It's not a lot of things, and somehow, the so many other things it IS, make up for that. It is a good place. A decent place. A clean place. A fair place. I know the lay of the land. I know the people. I know where things are. It is very simple here and, for whatever reason, it has made me keep coming back for more. I think it's the greatest city in the world...and I have seen a lot of the world. Calgary is that grand and glorious. I like the cold. I like the snow. I like the blue that lifts winter away. New York has everything but a sky. You'd miss that—I know I would. I should let the cat in.

I went into town yesterday to go to a movie and I passed a deer, crumpled up dead on the road. It was bent in half, its neck twisted behind its shoulders. I shuddered at the sight of her.

Timothy Findley died. I didn't know. I always wanted to meet him and tell him that he wrote my favourite book. I'll never get the chance now. I should have tucked a note in that poor deer's ear to take up to him...next time.

ja

Hailing A Limo
November 14, 2002

    I have a lot to do today. Shrodie is out sitting in the driveway squinting into the sun. He won't come in until his little paws lose all feeling. Somebody puked. It wasn't me. Living is weird.

ja

Dressed To Win
November 18, 2002

I have a gig up in Edmonton, so I thought I'd stay the extra day and see the Grey Cup game. We'll need to bundle up, I do know that. Those poor bastards looked frozen solid on the TV today. I am going to pray for snow so it will make us look very tough and rugged for the Americans tuning in (all five of them). Shania is playing at halftime and I know she will be an absolute blast to behold. If her torso is out, I'll know she really is Canadian. It would be the most depressing halftime entertainment in the history of the game: "I Would Die for You" followed by a rousing rendition of "Hanging By a Thread"... At least Shania has a bit of pep to her. Ahhh, if only I could write something with a bit of a beat...

I went to Mom and Dad's for dinner. She made some fucking great brownies for desert. She announced to Dad and me that there was a cup of butter and two cups of sugar in them. Dad said that she was trying to kill him. She laughed. "I am

on the verge of being diabetic," he said. She laughed some more. Sinister really. I think he had two.

My mom also said she thought my bum looked firmer. Whose mother says that? She said it twice. I laughed about that. "My bum?" I said. "Yes, your bum," she said. I told her that I had been lifting weights and she reached up and grabbed my arm and gave it a good squeeze. My dad then said that I was the healthiest, sturdiest singer in Canada. Oh my God, did I laugh in my head at this point. Never a dull moment—and they don't think they're funny.

jann

My Lord
November 19, 2002

We, my mother, my father and I, drove up to the peniten-
tiary yesterday afternoon to see my brother. Once again, it
was a humorous ride to say the least. My mother proceeded
to tell me about a squirrel-proof bird feeder that my dad had
made. It consisted of a long metal bar with a jar of some kind
attached to the top of it. The long metal bar will not permit
said squirrel's little hands from getting a little grip and making
his way up to the birdie num-nums. My dad, having complet-
ed his prototype, settled in to watch the results. My parents
quietly peered out the family room window, waiting for the
birds to flock down from the heavens. Alas, instead, with
great stealth, came the furry demon—a very large, fat, black
squirrel made his way to the new attraction and immediately
scampered quickly up the bar to the jar filled with bird seed.

My dad threw out a few God damns and a couple of
Jesuuuusss Christs and flew out the back door with a bottle of
vegetable oil (I am afraid to go on, but I must). He poured
some oil into an old cloth and began to lube up the metal bar,
foiling any more attempts by the squirrel to secure food for
what is sure to be a long, cold winter (I am trying to create
some drama here). Again, my parents waited with baited
breath by the window in the family room for birds to soar
down for a feast. And again, the big, fat, Greek wedding
squirrel ran toward the feeder with great anticipation. He
leapt onto the bar, clung for a brief moment and began his
slide down to the ground. My mother said that they laughed
for an hour watching that squirrel trying to figure out what
had happened to his technique. She said, "You have to come
over Jann and watch that squirrel try and get up there. It's
hilarious!"

j

A Prayer For Justin
November 26, 2002

It is not often that a person gets the chance that you are getting and that is to start all over again. Sometimes life seems so very strange that all we can really hang onto is change itself. You are about to embark on a great and glorious journey, one that's filled with hope and opportunity, joy and triumph, gladness and comfort. You will be filled with such enormous, eternal love, that one would need dark glasses from time to time just to gaze into it.

You are now turning a corner in what would seem to be your own destiny and you see, young Justin, you can change

destiny, but your fate, I am afraid, you are stuck with. This is your fate, this was always your fate, this was always your road. God is so big that he found you in this mess of a world and knew that you would need three angels to guide you through the fires that lick at our heels for 8oty or so years.

You are loved. You will be loved by all that meet you. You will succeed where others can only dream of succeeding. You will take life by the tail and swing her about your head. You will sleep so soundly that silence will be your blanket and your company. You will run in white sand with your pink new feet and laugh all day long. You will hold good things close to your heart and know that they are true and real. You will smile in the face of all evil and win every battle. God lies at the alter of your tiny body. You are on an adventure that circles the universe, every star and planet and every other world one could ever dream up.

You have been found, Justin. You have been found. You have been found and you will never be lost again. You are blessed and saved and you shall never fear loneliness or hunger or thirst. Love is your life. Kerry, Keaton and Beverly are your soldiers. We shall meet again and again and again. Welcome to the world.

j

Punctuation
December 8, 2002

I put my tree up with my friend. It was odd doing it on the first of December, but I am not going to be there any time soon, so I thought it best to get it up and decorated so I could forget about Christmas for the time being. The tree is fake, from Costco, one hundred and thirty nine dollars. Looks real enough. The cats have tried eating it and they found out quickly that a plastic needle coming out of their asses was a bit more painful than a little dry dead one. Where did Christmas come from all of a sudden??? It has certainly rushed in like a flood. A period that came two weeks early, if you ask me. And to top it off, you've got white jeans on. Well, I do. I always seemed to have white pants on when it really mattered. Shit. God help me. I am not sure that is what I wanted to say about Christmas.

On a happier note, I am recording for a new record. It should be good. Or not... Who the hell knows what could happen between here and there. I do the best I can do and that has to be good enough, my pretties. I should be finished by the end of February. I think it will be a cross between Kate Bush and Bush. I am kidding of course. Maybe more like a fat Calista Flockhart and a skinny Aretha Franklin. Hey, maybe even Ben Franklin and Franklin Roosevelt. Why did I do those mushrooms???

jann

Nikki's Birthday
December 9, 2002

It is Nikki's birthday today. She is thirty. I cannot believe that we have been working together for 5 years! She has been a godsend to me. Her dignity and grace and humour and intelligence never cease to amaze all of us around her. We are lucky indeed to have a leader that really truly cares about her work and how her decisions affect us all. I have never met a smarter woman. Never. She will look for a missing dime in the books for three days. Not many would. I am so grateful for you Nikki. Your ethics are bar-none, the stuff from which legends are made. We at J.A. Tours are extremely proud of you. I hope you have another hundred happy years on the planet.

The recording is going really well. It is amazing to think we have done 8 songs in 3 days. I can't get my head around it, but that is indeed the case. The boys are playing their hearts out. (By 8 songs, I mean the basic bed tracks that usually consist of bass and drums). It is the skeleton on which the rest of the song hangs. VERY important. The rest of the stuff I will be doing in my house. Piano, guitars, strings, percussion, vocals, etc... I have never worked like this before, but having Russell with me makes it all so easy. He knows what he is doing, whereas I do NOT.

I always miss my gram just that little bit more this time of year...this will be the 3rd Christmas? God I don't even know. What does that mean? Time is sealing up the cracks. It always does. People go. That's what we do. We come and we go. There is something so very lovely about it all.

j

Shame
December 11, 2002

Shame is a terrible and wicked thing. It can steal your very life out from under you. Shame is a shadow that follows you into the ladies room. Nothing will flush and you can't find a plunger. I have been ashamed many times in my life. I have felt the burning in my lungs and heart and stomach. I have been forced to lie down and cry it out of me in silence.

Silent crying is the saddest. To stand in a shower and let the water fall over you like a memory. You watch time drain in circles around your toes, down and away forever. You wait for the days to tick by, until the pressure lets up and the air begins to fill back into your defeat. I have been ashamed many times in my life. I know I shall be ashamed again at some point. It is a militant boot-camp teacher.

When the day breaks again tomorrow, I shall remain hopeful of better times, truer hearts, sharper minds. Kindness is a beacon for all of us to walk towards, run towards, arms flailing, hair blowing, sun shining. This is a good day to read Emily Dickinson and pray a little bit harder.

jann

Good Start
December 17, 2002

I am sitting here listening to Russ play guitar. We finished recording the bed tracks in Vancouver and now we are working out of my house doing everything else. I cannot tell you how wonderful it is to get up, work out and then just flop down on the couch and start working. I don't have to drive anywhere, be anywhere or go anywhere but here. Russ has dragged everything but the kitchen sink into my basement and so it is, that we are making music out of it all. I don't even know how to turn the computer on, never mind record anything. Thank Dog for him.

The phone is ringing...I shall not pick it up. It is probably my mother saying, "Pick up Jann." She thinks I can hear her. I should go and yell at Rusty. He is so amazing on that gee-tar. It is a marvel to watch him play.

ja

Bargains
December 25, 2002

No snow and no sign of snow ever again. Where is the snow? Where are the snow blowers? There are purple flowers frozen to their vine just a foot away from me. They are intensely cold. I can hear whispers of pure angst coming from every petal. They didn't even have time to fall off onto the ground to become dirt again. They look crucified, if you ask me. Good time of year for that I suppose...er, maybe that's Easter, isn't it?

Yes, the Lord our God, the One up there, the One and only All, Him, He, I AM, left out of the holidays again this year. He may have many names, but I am quite convinced at this time in my life, that He is one and the same by any name you want to call The Guy, Being, Entity.

The fighting that goes on over the Lord defies logic. We all know it does, yet we all continue the good fight to be right. My God is the right and only God. He will defeat you as you have the untrue God, the God that is false. We have a book to prove it. It's the same book! Religion will be our end. Spirituality will be our beginning. We have no leader in men. We have only people wanting to be right, not just, but right. Saddam the prince of the little weak people he has made, George the warrior, Blair the follower, Chrétien the empty-headed. We have no leaders.

I have said this before: do you want to be right, or do you want peace?? Because being right has absolutely no room in this world. Who will be the judge of what is right? Apparently, it's the guy with the biggest gun, the biggest army, the most tanks who inevitably becomes right.

There have been times in my life when being right was the hardest thing in the world to be. It cost me too much. I would much rather have peace now and let everyone else be right. I don't have the time in me anymore. I don't have to be anything but calm and peaceful. Right???

We must not measure each other. We must not compare ourselves to others. We must not want others to be like us. We must be able to stand alone. That is the only way we can stand together. All Gods. All people. All life. Precious and tender and fallible. Be tolerant. Be forgiving. Never judge a people by their leader. Never. People are good; leaders of the people are arses at the moment.

j

Snow Day
December 29, 2002

It snowed, finally. My dad was here this morning shovelling my driveway; hat half off his head, red ears, frozen breath. He said that he needed the exercise. Don't we all, after the eating going on around this place? If I ever see another piece of shortbread... People are skating on the lake. It looks very much like a Hallmark moment outside my window; scarves and gloves and long warm socks from Santa.

Shrodie is sleeping in my old paisley chair, it's his newest spot. He has rabbit feet today, big and long and white. The cats are all stir-crazy. They want it to be summer again. Little do they know that we are in for another 6 months of cold blue skies. My dad built them the biggest "cat-scratcher" in the history of the world. He brought it in with Russ's help on Christmas Eve. It is 5 feet high, with 3 rooms, stairs, doors, you name it. It is awesome. The cats have been having a riot in there. I threw some catnip in and all hell broke loose. Oh well, we all need to have a cheap laugh on occasion. It is quite amazing and somehow very funny all at once. It is completely carpeted with what looks like my mother's living room carpet??? I'll have to ask her, or maybe I shouldn't.

I have to go, as Russ is here and we are recording today.

jann

So Deeply
December 31, 2002

It's so quiet here. Shrodie is in the same spot it seems that he was a few days ago. I wish I were him 3 days out of the week.

God screws the lid onto another jarful of time and sets it upon a shelf in his room. He needs to change the sheets on His bed. It's hard when you are alone like Him. Things get neglected, like planets and children and wars.

A boy is skating out there on the lake. No, there are two of them, circling and falling and getting up. That's what life is some days. There are so many things that I want to stop circling. I want to just stand still and count clouds and make phone calls to myself, but not THIS self, another younger one who didn't think so much about it all. Not today I won't, stop thinking, that is. I thought all through my sleep and I am tired this morning. I need a drink of water.

I don't want to go out tonight, but I will. I have made promises again. If I had my way, I would never leave here. I would watch TV and look out of this window. Occasionally, I would read a book and eat something. I would wear a loose dress with flowers on it and brew tea. I would have long hairs poking out of my chin that the neighbour children would be frightened of... I would not wear my teeth. I would not return calls. I have 45 years to wait...

Imagine a peaceful world, the smiles of contentment on every continent. They said "never again" in 1945 and now here we are on the brink of yet another disaster. We don't like to remember how cruel we are. How mean. How wicked. How evil. Oh mercy. Let there be a year of no fighting. No loss. No blood spilling over little hands. Oh mercy, find us here and do not turn the light on; but let us sleep until we know better of ourselves. Do the best you can. Be good and kind and unclench your hands. We are together in this. So we shall remain, no matter what the outcome. What I do to you, I do to myself. Have a better year than last, that is my wish for you. Stand up.

j

Hold The Ice
January 7, 2003

We are finished the record. Well, but for a few dabs of paint here and there, it's a done deal. Russ and I will mix it in February at a little studio somewhere; someplace close to a coffee shop and a bowling alley. We will need to relax and drink caffeine, or vice versa. I think it's fantastic (not bowling, the record) but hey, what do I know? I wrote the thing, so how is one able to step back and see the shit pile when you are sitting on it? I just know what I like; I do not claim to know what's good.

It is so warm here that it's a bit like a horror movie. I don't know why. It is summery. It is January. It is weird to say the least. It was 15 degrees celsius yesterday. The lake will be melting from the bottom up; that's when it gets really unstable. I wouldn't save someone if they were to go in; I know I wouldn't. I'd call the AMA. Wait, that can't be right? Jumper cables???? AA? That's not it. Don't need recovering alcoholics out there fishing out children, now do we?

Well, I had best get going here. I am meeting Mom and Dad and going to Costco.

ja

Late Night
January 9, 2003

I am waiting for my parents to pick me up. We leave for somewhere tonight at midnight. I want to go to bed to tell the truth. I don't want to be flying all night. Oh will the glamour ever end??? They are always picking me up one way or another. That's what parents do; they pick you up and carry you over the slippery spots, the jagged rocks that rip away at little hands and knees.

Something is wrong with my fireplace. It is making a moaning noise and I mean a fairly loud one. Do fireplaces have fan belts? Someone is dying on the TV...or it could be a love scene. Hard to tell these days where the pain ends and the pleasure starts. That's entertainment.

It's good to cry over nothing, despite what they tell you. To cry over nothing will keep you on your feet. I feel so bad about Duray (new thought apparently). What it must be like to be in there. I hate visiting for 3 hours, never mind 25 years of pacing and dreaming of who you once were. I remember him so clearly. He was such a strong, handsome fellow. He had thick hair with a little white patch at the crown. I don't even know if he's still got that. I'll look next time. He called me the other day and said that his computer quit. He said he wanted to just die. He said he felt dead anyhow. I pray he gets out. Somehow. Someday.

The universe is SO big, eh?

j

Tropical Moons
January 14, 2003

Last night was altogether another story. Picture the entire band and crew naked in a small illuminated pool somewhere in Jamaica. Yes, all of us, the whole damn gang nekkid and floating around in our "private" pool. We laughed so hard, that I felt quite sick this morning. My new name is Boob Marley. There are pictures that I really need to have destroyed. And to think the whole thing was my idea. How much did I drink? You really don't want to know...that's why I don't drink!!!!

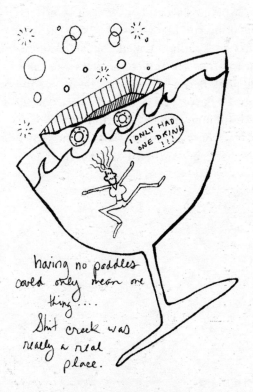

There is a LOT of pot on this island. They want you to buy it at every turn, "Lady, you know me?? You want to buy some pot man?" I say NO and that I am a police officer. That puts an end to the conversation. I don't know what the going rate for pot is, but you can buy a bail of it here for 3 dollars. I mean a giant pile of pot for a few loonies. What is the world coming to? I think if they shipped a few boatloads to old Mr. Bush, we'd all be a bit better off. The guy is a tightwad, wound around his own ass furthermore.

Well, we are all sitting here outside the hut and watching the stars twinkle. It sounds corny, but it's so wonderful to hear the crickets and the talking and the wind through the trees and the water. It makes you feel all right for a second or two. Just a second or two, but a second or two that winds itself back into your soul, making you like yourself a little bit more. I am not a person that goes around naked...but it felt good to have my breasts and my toes out under the stars and under the water. You feel unencumbered by your own flesh. It somehow comes off of you and lets you feel light and a little sinful. I like feeling a little sinful now and again; I think we all do.

I miss my parents. I miss my cats. I miss my gram. I miss home all the time, even when I am there.

jann

All In A Day
January 19, 2003

I am home for a few hours. The cats are piled into the chair beside me here in my office. Once in a while, they like each other's company. Once in a while, they like my company. I know that they miss me when I am gone. I miss them.

I can't believe I am going to Mexico tomorrow. It's warm here. Not a single bit of snow. New houses everywhere. I hope Norah Jones wins everything at the Grammy's. I hope Diana Krall wins as well. I hope the world doesn't blow up. I hope people can bear each other for a few thousand more years. I need to repack. I think I heard the doorbell.

jann

No Jump
January 27, 2003

I have returned from the tropics. I need to rest from resting so damn much. The cats have circled me for hours now, wondering how long I will be home this time. Two weeks, I think? Anyhow, I am home and in my housecoat at 6:11 p.m. Wonderful. Marvellous. Fed the cats. Going to make chili, except I need onions. Who do you call for onions at 6:11 at night? My mother, who else? And my dad will be the one who brings them to me and he'll also bring a gravy boat with him that mother had on the counter to give to me, or something like that...maybe even a doily. We all need a good doily now and then (doily is a weird word).

Love to all,

j

Gobs Of Happiness
January 31, 2003

Happiness does not lie over any hill. It is not near, it is not close even, it is immediate. It is in you and on you; it already is. Just to be living is wondrous. We don't realize it until it's far too late. We have cancer, or we've lost our loves, or we drink it away, or we work too hard, or we blow it into the air in black puffs of smoke, it dangles like spit. My older brother used to hang over me, hair falling forward, laughing madly with spit dripping just barely above my eyes. I remember screaming and trying to free myself and then he would suck the long streaming gob back into his head and move on.

Happiness seems like that. Happiness was getting up off the floor. Happiness was and is that memory. There are so many good things. Remember them for the times when there seem to be none. The trees, the sky, the dirt under my nails are enough. Crying for others instead of yourself will make you happier. Sitting still and thinking of the earth spinning through all this magic will make you happier.

You are happy. You just don't know how happy you are. You are waiting for something to happen that says, "You are happy now." It will never happen. Only in the innocence of a moment will you see anything with any clarity. There are no steps to happiness. There are no secret doors to unlock. Well, maybe one secret door; to accept your life and to be satisfied with that in and of itself. Just being must be enough.

Envy will most certainly make you vain and bitter. To want to be what you are not will steal your sleep. Burn your magazines. Burn the ideas of others, embrace your own self and tell it that it's fine. I am fine. My body. My heart. My soul. My happiness is gold.

Happiness already is; you just can't see it because you want so much more. We should really be wanting so much less, but that's not what we're taught. We are taught to always want what everybody else has and I bet that it's not happiness. It's empty and blank, just like a disappointed face. A heart will beat even when a mind is dead. That is a good thing to remember. It speaks volumes about being human. A horse will run even if it's snapped a leg clear off, it has a huge heart that wants to keep running no matter what. That is a good thing to remember.

Oh God, have mercy on us all. Let me live to see a day when there is one white flag flapping gladly in the breeze. Oh God, have mercy on the people that lead us all from the red rocket skies into the freedom and bliss of acceptance. To live and let live is the only answer. But then, how will we eliminate those that take that right away? That is what is happening now...the line that is crossed and wiped out by hatred and greed.

Be happy now my dearests. This is all there is. Buy flowers. Sit and smile about what a glorious trip this is indeed! Even if we are all to die, right now we are living and that is all we can do. Live well. Enjoy your life; don't waste your precious moments worrying about what has not yet come.

jann

♥ equals ☮

Sheepless
February 5, 2003

I looked at the clock at 4:23 a.m. Wide awake, mind twirling around in tight little knots. I don't know why. One of the cats was sleeping soundly beside me. The bed was empty other than that. Shrodie brings me mice in the middle of the darkness; I had three wetly mauled ones lying neatly beside my left ear. I stared at the clock radio that my friend bought me for Christmas and watched the numbers change from 23 to 24 to 25 to 26 to 27 to 28... It was nearly 5:30 when I last remember seeing them flicker on to the next digit. I think that sometimes I am not well, that my mind has its own little body and it leaves me staring at clocks from time to time.

To do too little means the death of the heart. Perhaps the pin is pointed when you abandon your expectations. Someday I will know what that really means. I say it, but I seldom know "it." What is an expectation anyway? It seems to me to be just more wanting and not really needing. It is a close cousin to hoping. Not much good that is either; too desperate for my taste.

I miss the snow. The white. The breaths you can see stream out of your nose and mouth. I miss Leonard and Dale. I miss my dog Aquarius and my gram. It's good to miss things and people. It makes you feel alive. It says, "here I am and here I go again." Nothing quite as sad as a person who misses nothing at all.

j

Dog Day Afternoon
February 9, 2003

I saw a dog yesterday, a gaunt Golden Retriever, wandering around frantically on Sarcee Trail here in Calgary. He was surely lost. I was in the far lane turning, so I couldn't hop out and grab the poor soul. You don't know how badly I wanted to. The dog edged closer and closer to the busy road, missing the racing cars by inches. I hit the horn in hopes of getting his attention. He never looked up, he just looked fearfully from side to side, trying to see something familiar, anything at all... It is hard to be lost. We all know what that's like, if only for a moment or two, we do know.

A van stopped briefly beside the dog and threw its door open. A woman hopped out and extended her hand to him, coaxing him away from the traffic. That dog started wagging his tail so hard I thought he would fall over. He was overjoyed with blind relief. She was trying to avoid seeing him hit by a car; she was trying to help. I was grateful to her. "Is this my person?" thought the dog. No it was not.

I had to turn the corner so I don't know what happened. I tried to peer out my side-view mirror and it looked as though the woman just got back into her van with the dog left on the curb. I don't know what came after that. I started to cry. Just a few tears seeped out of my head and I brushed them aside. I felt stupid somehow. I seldom blink an eye at some poor bastard drunk passed out on the street. I somehow don't care. I felt stupid about that as well.

What is it with the hardening of the heart? I care more about animals than people. People are so determined to ruin themselves that you almost have to sit back and let them. Whereas a dog or a cat or a horse, any living thing really, relies on our kindness and common sense. We are cruel though. We want to live out loud at the expense of every other living thing. I have days when I know that people are good, but that is swiftly replaced by thinking we are all evil the very next second. It all depends on what lies at our feet. Consistency would be a welcome friend as far as goodness goes. I hope that dog found his person. I hope we all find our person.

Russ just got here. We have two more things to lay down today for the new record and then...drum roll...we are finished this thing. We'll start mixing Wednesday in Vancouver. It's a terribly, profoundly, sad CD and I couldn't be happier about that. Sad and delicious. Sad and glorious. Sad and so very uplifting...to me anyway. I don't know how else to write for people if I don't do it for me first. Selfish, but very necessary. I am all over the place... I can't finish one thought. I have too many thoughts today. They are driving me mad.

j

Who's Counting
February 13, 2003

I don't have much time to write, as I am off to see about getting my shoulder fixed. I don't know how I managed to screw it up as badly as I have, but that is indeed the case. I can hardly lift myself into a bra (don't picture that). I can hardly move the thing—my shoulder not my boob. Perhaps I should not have lifted that car off of the Brownie troupe...don't you think that would have been a good idea???? Kidding. I have just said the word "don't" three times. Make that four. I am still Jannie from the block...I don't know what that means. Make that five times.

I am mixing the record with Russ. It's going to be fantastic, if I may say so myself. Perhaps I will be the only sap that likes it, but that would be alright too. I don't understand MuchMusic. I have been watching it for a half hour and I think everything and everyone looks completely nuts. Music and the music business are terrible bedfellows. They make oil and water look like lovers.

j

Listening
February 17, 2003

There is a fear brewing inside of me, a big one, a fierce one. I don't know quite how to describe its size or its origin; it was just suddenly upon my heart. Things are changing in my life so quickly that I, for the most part, cannot catch my breath. I feel it get caught in my teeth on its way out of my lungs. I think about every breath and it's maddening. What is life? What is life?

I wake up 4 or 5 times wondering where my sleep has gone. I am not sleeping well at all. I am thinking that I won't get to sleep, so therefore, I do not. I roll over and over inside of sheets that seem to strangle my legs. Twisting like a fox in a metal trap. I wish I could chew a leg off just to get some bloody sleep.

I have so much mail to return. I look at my computer and don't know where to start, so therefore, I do not. I feel fine physically, tired, but for all the right reasons. My mind has a

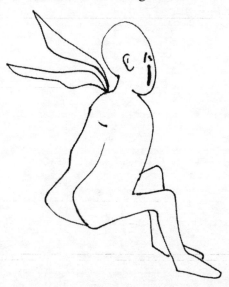

spark. I am wondering what and who is next? I am looking so far ahead of myself, that I have created a bit of a monster. Perhaps this has been a long time coming.

Change, in order to be effective, must be radical. My heart has wings and they are fluttering and making my legs ache. My legs ached so badly last night...they kept me up even longer than usual. I am aching all over. It is a drone that I can almost hear. Interesting. I am wondering. I am thinking and pondering and napping on the leather couch in the studio thinking about my life. Listening to my head talk to my heart and hoping it never ends.

jann

Rain, Rain Go Away
February 19, 2003

We have seven songs mixed. Seven. It all sounds dreamy and sad eyes. It sounds like a heart in a Tiffany blue box. It sounds like my own life walking down an old, lonesome, dirty road. My friend Beth dropped in on me today. She is so big eyed and looking out into the vast plain of the universe. She and I don't need to talk; I can tell by just looking at her how she feels and what she wants to say. Music is hard on her heart, I fear. It takes her up too high, where it's hard to breathe. She is so small on the outside and so big on the inside; I love that about her.

j

Changes
February 20, 2003

I feel happy today. We are nearly done the record. Russell and I go from cheering out loud, to hanging our heads in disbelief. When you are done with something, that means you must, indeed, move on. You cannot stand still in life; it will not let you. You try to, but it will not let you. I feel happy, although I do not know what that means.

I should go. I have a lot going on and I don't know where it stops or starts or if I even want it to.

j

Acting Lessons
March 6, 2003

I am back in my new LA hotel room. We had to move this morning as I was mortified by the hotel we were in. What it was is beyond me. More like a casting call...I have to tell you that it was weird-o-rama. I think my room was in the middle of the bar. That's how noisy it was. Maybe I was too tired to think as we flew in from a 17-hour stay in New York, but I doubt that was the problem. The lobby looked as though the Village People had been drunk in it for years and had been continually decorating. There was a glass room behind reception that had a half-nude woman typing on her Apple computer...whatever. Good part-time job to put her through acting classes, I suppose.

The record is now finished. I don't know whether to laugh or cry. Niks and Russ and I went for sushi and now I am in my new hotel room listening to what we have done these past three months. I do want to cry. I don't think the CD will be out till September; which is fine I guess. It will give me time to get up, wake up and stand up. It seems like I am on another planet most moments. I am tired. That must be it. All this flying is very, very glamorous. I should go to bed. I sound like a bloody fool. Maybe because I am one.

j

Things To Do
March 11, 2003

    The snow has covered everything in the yard. My lights are buried and cast an eerie glow when the sun goes down. I didn't know what they were at first; little flying saucers, fallen stars, a lost car...

jann

A Bit Off
March 12, 2003

It seems brighter around here today. I still don't feel all that well. I am just kind of breathing in and breathing out. That's all you can do for the most part. The sky is bright, the snow is white and I have puke to clean off of the top of the stairs leading into the basement. Someone, it seems, threw up Michigan. Fuck.

I took a couple of Tylenol PMs last night and that seemed to dull my headache and put me to sleep until about 4 a.m. Sweet Pea was tucked in beside me like a Latin lover (are they that hairy?).

Should go and have a bath...I'll stare up through the skylight and look for signs of good things to come. I am so grateful for all that I have. I have too much. I do try to give it away and it always comes back...go figure.

jann

Voice Of Many
March 13, 2003

The human condition is vast and wide. It is complicated and so very simple all at the same time. We all find ourselves asking the same questions. Why, being the biggest one of all. It drives us mad that we cannot know why. You get pieces of the answer all your life. You get to see glimpses of miracles. You have to watch so closely though, or you'll miss them altogether.

Hope is never lost; it waits in our hearts like a floating feather. Or, it sits there like a stone, weighing us down. Hope is many things—it can lift you and sink you. Remember that. There is a time to abandon it.

j

NOT
KNOWING
=
LEARNING
EVERYTHING

All Quiet
March 17, 2003

The quiet is what seems to be the most startling. The quiet and the time that goes by so slowly, it makes your heart ache. The stillness of thinking about a future that is not to be, that will not be, that cannot be. I watched dust drift through rays of sunlight this morning. I followed a single cat hair floating up towards my face. I blew it away. I drank water and turned the channels on the TV. I didn't watch anything at all. I took a bath with lavender salts and made it far too hot. I was out of breath just lying there in it. I felt my heart beating and I counted them as they went by. My face was red along with my hands and my feet and my pretty much everything else. I had to lie on the bed stark naked to cool down. I thought I might keel over. I hoped that my parents didn't burst through the front door with the carpet shampooer (one never knows around here).

It made me tired, or was it relaxed? Hard to tell on a day like today. I wish it were colder. It is warm here and soft and melting like a cone in the back of an open pickup truck. I remember being 10 years old and licking ice cream off of my arms and my legs in the back of my dad's rusty yellow work truck. He was speeding along Old Banff Coach Road and I was trying to salvage what was quickly becoming a liquid mess. It was a tiger ice cream, orange and licorice, my favourite. I think we had gone to Cochrane for something or the other and Dad had treated us to cones at MacKay's ice cream parlour. They made fantastic ice cream. Maybe they are still there. I'll drive out sometime this summer and see for myself.

Mom and I made it through the jail visit without any problems. I mean NONE. Neither of us tested for anything. Had we, I might have cried as we both went to such great lengths to swab the decks as it were. We had our ID in zip-lock bags.

We brought a wet washcloth to wipe our coats and hands and keys and faces and glasses. We did everything we could to not be "chemically challenged." We were nervous. Mom told me not to talk to them if they didn't talk to me. She told me that I was just like Dad and that my temper was terrible. That's when I punched her...kidding. Anyhow, the guards couldn't have been nicer if they tried—which seemed odd to my mother and me. I mean nicer than we have ever been treated there in all these years. Hhhmmmm??? We usually are made to wait in this little "holding area" until our names are cleared, or something like that and then we are led into the building where the visits are held. Yesterday, they said, "Oh no, you guys can go straight in."

I looked at Mom and she looked at me and off we staggered over the 4-inch deep slush.   When we pulled up to the parking lot, we saw Duray on the Bobcat clearing snow.   It reminded me of better days when Duray's son would sit up on his lap, on Duray's Bobcat and whirl around. They had such fun on that thing. Fuck, they are hard to drive. Try it sometime, nearly impossible.

We went into the visiting area and were immediately approached by a guard who said, "Miss Richards, your brother is going to be a bit late, as he was working today."   I looked at Mom and she looked at me like we had both lost our nuts. I have NEVER had anyone tell me he would be late.   We have sat in that room for 45 minutes and had to go up to the "cage" to inquire about Duray's whereabouts.   Not yesterday. Weird.   Odd.   I wonder why?

If only everyone could be treated like that all the time, we'd really be onto something.   We felt like real people with real hearts and real heads and real lives.   We didn't feel like prisoners for a change. We felt respected. We respected them right back. That is how it works. You do not demand respect, you earn it. It is SO hard to go in there and face it all on a good day, on a bad day, I cannot even tell you of the terror.

Shrodie is snoring.   I am drinking Dr. Pepper.   I should get the hell out of this house before I pull my own molars out. It's just too damn quiet.   I've got too many clocks ticking away in here.   Why do I have all these damn clocks?

The name of my new CD is going to be *Love Is The Only Soldier*. Fitting really.   That's all the information I have.

jann

Rolling Along
March 20, 2003

I had some oatmeal this morning, well this afternoon. It's supposed to be good for something, is it not? Oh, and never mind that, after doing my "duty" to God, Queen and country just now, I realized all too late that there was NO toilet paper anywhere to be seen. I considered the cardboard roll and then just decided to "hop" to the guest bathroom, upstairs no less...I was quite the sight I must say. And the fact that I am telling you is further proof that fame is nothing short of glamour, glamour, glamour...

ja

STORY OF MY LIFE

B&B
March 21, 2003

Everyday is so, well, new. What a profound thought! I sit here looking out this window and wonder how it is that not so far around the world, it is night and bombs are dropping like rain drops. So many theories as to why now? None of them accurate I am afraid. We will never really know the "how comes," and the "what fors." That is for others to know. I just heard somebody die...

I'm tired today. Went to see my pal Bif Naked last night. She went on at midnight...my God, I should have worn my p-jays! It was a really great, loud, high-energy show. She is a terrific writer. She is a terrific person. So down to earth and good hearted and I am proud to be her friend. We met last year at the Junos and have kept in close contact ever since. I just love her. Her kindness is something you don't expect. I am sure people assume that her music makes her a hard drinking, pill-popping rocker. Not so. She is so full of peacefulness and love and serenity. She is a gem. I have never seen anyone work as hard as she does. I had fun watching the night unfold. It was good to see her face. Safe travels, honey...

I think my ears are still ringing, or maybe that was the phone? Her fans went nuts; standing on shoulders and waving arms and smashed together like a bunch of potatoes. People were spraying beer and body surfing...just like at my shows.

j

Seen The Wind
March 23, 2003

The wind can be maddening. It seems to drive even the trees crazy. They keep trying to be upright and straight and still. It is impossible. Their heads snap around like neglected dolls. I don't like the wind; in fact, I hate it. I find it distracting. It will ruin a perfectly good baseball game. It will massacre a picnic, blowing paper plates and plastic forks and spoons and cups across the fields. If you have children to run after them it's fine, otherwise, your appetite is lost. Bits of dirt will find their way into the fried chicken and the rice pudding and the cold lemonade.

The wind can ruin any good party. My friend Kerry was swept up by a tent and dropped in the neighbour's yard two summers ago. She forgot to let go of the pole. She broke two ribs. The wind did that to her. She couldn't speak for hours. The wind got into her lungs and stole her voice.

I hate the wind. The wind will blow clouds into your eyes on a perfectly good summer day. It will blow the sun over the hills hours before it's supposed to set. It will whip hair into your mouth and stripe it with wet balls of gob. You pull it out of the side of your parched lips, but it's too late, it's already damp and clumped together. Then the wind sends your hair crashing into the corners of your eyes, the sting and the burn and grit. The wind will keep a paper bag in the air for hours, making it do a crazy dance that it does not wish to do. The bag is hypnotized and mesmerized and haunted into every single move (poor old bag).

I hate the wind. It will blow skirts up over the heads of schoolgirls and nuns. It will make waves steal sand from the shore. It will crash buses full of old ladies on vacation over cliffs and through guardrails, all those pairs of broken glasses and missing shoes.

I hate the wind. The only souls that like the wind are those of dogs. When there is no wind to be found, they will beg for a car ride and stick their heads out as far as they can go to find it, ears flapping, tongues wagging. Dogs love the wind. They are the only ones. The wind will break your heart if you let it. It will ruin your concentration. It will keep you up at night. It will turn your trailer over and kill the family cat. Nobody likes the wind. I hate the wind.

j

Proud Sponsors Of This Journal
March 28, 2003

I am drinking Neo Citran. I have a cold or perhaps just am being attacked by phlegm. Clouds are rolling through my sinuses. They are about to rain down on my throat and pour out of my eyes. Whatever it is, it's here and it's in my body to stay for a while. I do need the company though. I like Neo Citran; it's like a liquid nap.

I think I'll just stay in tonight and watch TV. It's hard to find a station that doesn't have the war smashing about on it. Poor old world. Poor people. Poor families. Poor old world. I could not be any more confused if I was...well, more confused. I know I cannot change the world, so I'll have to just keep trying to change myself... I wonder when the DVD box set of the war will be available on the home shopping network??? I am confused. I don't know what to think. I can actually say that I do not know what is right anymore. I find that horrifying. Enough said.

I didn't sleep that well. My friend's phone phoned my phone late last night and I couldn't get back to sleep after that. All I could hear was rave music and people yelling at each other. I know they weren't at a Weight Watchers meeting...at least, I think they weren't. You worry about people when their phones phone your phone. I have now said the word phone too much. I listened to the music blasting for a few minutes and then felt too voyeuristic to continue the very one-sided conversation. What if something nasty had been said about me? What then? (I have a weird imagination).

My Neo Citran is cold in my cup. I am going to lie on the couch and watch the world. I may even say a prayer and send it out as far as my heart will take it. Praying never hurts, unless you actually expect an answer right off the bat. You have to wait and really look and listen, and lo and behold, tiny beads of wisdom come pouring into your body, and for a moment or two, you can bathe in the relief of knowing for certain that you are not alone.

j

Spring Cleaning
April 2, 2003

Depression is a precious thing in small doses. It makes you appreciate the good times, the easy times, the funny times. It makes you appreciate time itself.

j

Hobby Time
April 3, 2003

    I have spent most of my life writing about love. Where it might be found, how it would be lost, why it would not return, when it might strike one down? My whole life spent wondering about it, looking at it, chasing it, dreaming about it, praying for it, pondering whom it is exactly. I don't regret a moment. A friend of mine once told me that it is better to run into the sunrise than into the sunset and I think he's right. You know when people talk endlessly about walking into the

sunset??? Why is that? The sunset will not give you the day back, whereas the sunrise holds nothing but promises of a full day ahead. I like that sentiment. I like that a lot. I want to walk into the sunrise from now on.

Oh the heartache of love...it is heartache that makes us all fall down. It is the road that we as human beings must plod over for miles and miles until our lives end. That is the condition we find ourselves in. Not an unfair one, but simply one that makes our world exist. We are put here to love one another. We will look until we can look no more. We seldom need to be able to see, just feel our way through.

As I get older, I believe less and less in a "soulmate." I think now that we can have many "soulmates" in our lives. Our friendships have got to be just as important as our lovers, our others, our partners, as it were. Our friendships are soulmates on a grand scale. They travel through time with us, through pain with us, through all that could and does go wrong with us. Friends are our weightless saviours whom we lean on and fall on and walk on from time to time. They do not forsake us, ever. Sex screws up many a good friendship. Sexuality, the curse, perhaps, that sends a friendship into the abyss. Sex takes no time at all, where a friendship takes a lifetime. Think about that.

If you don't have a friend within your lover, then you in actuality have zilch. Sex is the most boring thing on the planet, yet that's what everything fucking revolves around. The selling of America is sex. The selling of the world is sex. A half-nude girl with milk on her lip...a Gucci purse dangling from the leg of a pubescent 12-year-old girl...a giant billboard of a crotch clad in a pair of white boys underpants...A car, a bunch of grapes, a new house, a chocolate bar, a diet plan. Lose weight, have sex, is basically what they feed you (no pun intended).

Sex is for people who have no hobbies. Sex is for people

who have no talents. Sex is the most overrated thing the world has or ever will witness. I mean that. I am so sick of sex. Sick of being asked about it. Sick of thinking about it, talking about it, having it thrown in my face day after day. Can SOMEBODY think of something a bit more interesting than sex? See what happens when you drink decaf? I am kidding for the most part, but you know what I mean: sex, sex, sex. It can be so great and so bloody terrifying. A guy is taking the Christmas lights off of that tree I was talking about a while ago. He looks quite sexy doing it.

jann

Outside In
April 8, 2003

Change in order to be effective, must be radical. That is what the famous, crazy, German philosopher Nietzsche once said. I have quoted him many times before. I always loved that saying. It's almost as good as Einstein's, great spirits have always encountered violent opposition from mediocre minds. How true indeed. The funny part about change is that nothing ever really changes. It just keeps circling the parking lot looking for a place to park.

All I know is that I want to be me and at the end of the day, that's a pretty darn good declaration of sorts. I don't want to be anybody else. I don't wish my life were different. I don't want anything, you see, I want everything. I want to know things. I want to wonder endlessly and hope eternally that what is out there is wonderful and colourful and gloriously kind. I can hear the TV upstairs. I like hearing the voices roll through the house like they were at the kitchen table playing Scrabble. I know that sounds pathetic and I don't mean it to. I like people; after all they do and are, I still like them. I still want to write about them and know them and understand them. Believe me, I have my days when I don't want a person within 56 miles of me. I don't feel like that today. I like liking someone. I like someone right now. This second. This instant. It's not me, but someone even better. It's you.

jann

Dinkity Winkity Wonkle Hoffer
April 11, 2003

I am drinking a carrot/apple juice. My mom and dad gave me a Waring juicer for my birthday and I love it. Carrots run when they see me coming. I bought a pineapple that I am going to try and cram in there later on in the week (I'll cut it into wee pieces, don't worry).

All of the snow is gone. The only thing that shows itself now is this godawful orange grass that looks so thirsty and fed up really, from winter shutting itself off and on. Who could blame it? I would not want to be a blade of grass in this part of the world. I can still see remnants of colour clinging to dried flowers...purple and pink and bright yellow. I wonder what it would taste like crumbled up on a salad? I'll have to try that sometime, or try it out on somebody else is more like it.

I can hardly wait for everything to start poking itself up through the dirt. I never thought I would love to watch a garden, but I do. I walk about the yard all summer long and gaze at the little darlings stretching themselves up towards the sun. I haven't a fuck of a clue what anything is called and I don't care to. I love the ones who can pace frantically through a patch of growing things and name everything off. "Well here we have the dinkity winkity wonkle hoffer...and this is the duchess coolge mine hearted spleen spiggle." "Ahhhhh, I see," is all I can muster. Then I am told that the "dinkity winkity wonkle hoffer would fare much better out of the sun."

My mom is always moving my plants around when I am away because of just that. "This plant needs direct sun, Jann" she'll say...or "My God Jann, have you ever watered this poor plant?" They are perched up on tables and chairs and moved from floor to floor. I never know where the hell my plants have gone. I'll just suddenly notice one on top of the TV in my bedroom and think to myself, my God, the woman has lost her marbles!

I remember my mother telling me a great fairy tale about a bleeding heart plant. I forget how it went. I should phone her up and ask her about that. I just thought about it this second. I like remembering old things, well, as long as they are the good old things, the bad old things can ruin a perfectly good meal. Oh, the splendour of a tree! What would this world look like without a single tree rooted into its sides? Very terribly, horribly sad indeed.

I think I am moving from here this year. I won't miss it. I may miss looking out of this window, but it won't be for long. I'll have a new window to write about and look out of—and into, for that matter. My folks and I found a forest not far from here. It's a secret, wonderful forest with deer poop and horse hooves etched into the snow banks. The sun comes down in shards and hides amidst the thick bushes and ferns. I am enchanted by this place. My dad's face looked so young as we walked the property lines. I could see him thinking of a fishing rod and a campfire and a view of the mountains. His face was so calm and serene.

jann

Old Friends
April 14, 2003

The fog is resting on the still frozen water; the mists of Avalon, knights in armour and damsels in pointed white hats, fairies and princes and arrows with feathered ends. This is the sight in front of me. There is a light rain that makes every single thing look alive and well, although my lawn looks the colour of a red-headed stepchild, unwanted and unnoticed for the most part. It's hard not belonging to anyone. A few green leaves of some buried perennial are poking up through the soil on the north side of the house. I, of course, know not what they are, but nonetheless, they seem determined and hearty and steadfast.

I went to my friend Susan's last night for dinner. I haven't seen her in at least 10 years. We tried to figure out when indeed the last time was. She is unchanged, I mean she is surely "changed" as we all are after the passing of a decade, but her face and her eyes were the same shining things they were in high school. She just looked radiant. We sipped on some Argentine wine and ate shrimp and talked about who we were once and wondered where everybody else had disappeared to...

Susan said the nicest thing to me; this too I shall make a note to remember and put away with my other precious things. She said, "Finding an old friend was like finding a lost piece of treasured jewellery." It made me blush almost. I felt my cheeks fill up with an odd kind of gratefulness. When people mean what they say, the words permeate all doubt and all time and all fear.

jann

Happy!
April 29, 2003

I have not written a word in weeks. My life, it seems, has run off and left me. I have not stopped moving and I am tired beyond words. Maybe that's why I can't seem to write any of them down. Maybe I shouldn't be writing when my head is like this. I can picture everything. I can feel everything. I can hear every word that was ever said.

Shrodie is humping his blanket. For a guy with no balls, he can still do a pretty convincing hump. I like it when he bites a corner of the blanket like an old lover. What a nut. I'll have to try out a few of his moves on somebody...Yeah, right.

I am going to go put on pyjamas and watch the lake. I have the house to myself. My friend from England was here for a wee visit...we had a blast. The boys were here for rehearsal...getting ready for NY. The snow had Darcy and Lyle stranded on the highway for 30 hours. Anyhow, lots going on here the past week. My house was full of men...nothing new, eh? Usually it's just my dad wandering about replacing light bulbs (my life is exciting, you just wouldn't believe it really).

j

What If
April 30, 2003

I didn't sleep last night. I hate that. The pillows felt like little vicious enemies pulling at my hair. I finally got up and roamed around with the cats, playing computer Scrabble and drinking water. My head is swimming in the muck of a far too busy life. I don't know what to pack. I don't know what I want to eat. I don't know what thought to put out there first and deal with today. The sun is so bright that you'd think it would burn away all this mental fog...not so.

I leave on Friday for our New York adventure. I worry every second that no one will show up for these gigs. It'll be like Smithers, British Columbia in 1984, when I sang in a bar with 3 loggers and a couple of native girls and the bartender looking on...We got requests all night for "Aqualung" and "Dust in the Wind." Good bloody hell. We knew the song "Cocaine" by Jackson Browne and a couple of Foreigner tunes. We were the worst fucking band to ever live, I swear.

MY CAREER

ME

What if no one shows up in New York? I wonder if I'll just cry myself awake at night or shrug it off like a bad date? Part of me knows it doesn't matter who is there, because I'll have my boys and we'll be playing music and that's all I really care about. Just the doing of that is so much. It fills your heart full of love. I wouldn't know what else to call it. It's pure love. On top of it all, CTV is shooting a documentary about my subsequent failure or success therein, (whatever the case may be) and that makes me almost sick. I say almost sick, because it's not going to be all that bad, I am just being dramatic. I have so many people helping me through it all...thank God.

jann

Time Of My Life
May 11, 2003

I am in New York. I am racing through every moment. I cannot catch my breath, or even find it to catch up with it, for that matter. It is everything all at once. New York is lit up and constant and eerie. We are playing upstairs at Studio 54 to 40ty or 50ty people every night, which I find to be a small miracle. I didn't expect anyone to be waiting for me when I lurched onto the stage on Wednesday night. I thought there would just be the bartender, a waitress and the film crew—that is following my every move to the point of exhaustion—sitting on little chairs drinking beer out of plastic cups.

I am having the time of my life. I feel weightless, like vapour, like steam, like a white cloud. I am up for the task of being on the planet and trying desperately to learn something along the way. I am waiting for the sky to open up and for Jesus Christ himself to come bursting into the room and tell me I've made it after all. I feel everything coming into me and I am letting it just pour itself back out. I have no idea what I am doing at any given moment. I have thrown myself onto the feet of the lions and am eager to watch the chips fall and fly where they may. Life is unpredictable and frustrating and all about waiting for signs of eternity.

j

So Much
May 16, 2003

This city is like a kiss. A kiss that makes you either want to weep uncontrollably, or jump through rings of fire screaming at the top of you lungs that you finally understand the meaning of life. The dirt and the filth smothered in the smell of coffee and dog shit and cotton candy and gasoline and Danish pastries. It's so much to take in all the time, 24/7, night and day, constant noise, honking, yelling, hollering ,homelessness. My ears are ringing from the speed at which this place moves. You hear it going by you when you lie in bed at night. You hear drunken souls spilling out of the Broadway shows, chatting about the plays and the stars and where they should all go to eat and drink some more.

Food is so abundant here that it smothers the streets, literally. It is everywhere. It is on every corner, in every building, in every head and mouth and tip of tongue. It is pouring out onto the streets and covered with French mustard and coleslaw. The buses are giant hot dogs with sweet onion and relish speeding through town in search of a cold pop. Everything here is food. It's all edible and delicious and intoxicating and drunk. I have staggered through the Village and pondered what indeed I should eat next. I usually pass by a hundred or so places before I can finally decide on a tuna sandwich or a cup of fruit with some almonds. I keep buying water and leaving it in some store where I have tried on yet another pair of shoes...

I keep looking up and bumping into groups of Asian people taking pictures of buildings and each other and of signs in Times Square. I say "sorry" all day long to people and poles and hydrants and cars that I smash into constantly from not looking where I am going. My jaw is dropped open wide, staring at people who are stranger than anything my imagination could ever conjure. They are so crazy and perhaps so sane, all at the same moment, that it leaves you pondering your own mental well-being.

My parents and my brother are coming today. I wish Duray could see this place. He would love it here. I can hear him giggle about all the "loonies" as he would call them, wandering around, eating food out of the garbage cans. I watched a woman pick half a sandwich off of a plate at an outdoor cafe yesterday. The person eating it of course had left, but it still left me feeling empty and selfish and grateful and shameful. It made me feel everything that a person shouldn't feel at 2 o'clock in the afternoon. She picked up that sandwich and bit into it like it was just part of another simple day on the planet, where one needs to fill one's soul and try to get themselves into yet one more morning.

jann

Kick At The Darkness—Part I
June 4, 2003

I am afraid today. Of what, I cannot really tell. It is a fear of going forward by myself and finding that there is nothing more than what there is. Human I guess. My body has memories in it that take my breath away. There are days I want to live over and over and over again. Life is amazing.

j

Kick At The Darkness—Part II
June 4, 2003

I keep thinking that I can be in a newly built house a year from now...impossible.   I can picture myself there 45 years from now, in an old purple-skid-marked housecoat. Watering plants, feeding birds and cats and squirrels and brewing tea and drinking whiskey out of a tin can. Floppy hat, sunglasses, moustache, beard...oh sweet Jesus. I'll be there wandering around, talking to myself and waiting for a car to drive up, any car. Even somebody lost that I can drag into the house to tell my tales to. I can't wait, but I will.

jann

Just Looking
June 14, 2003

Everything in my life is changing. I mean everything. I have so much on my mind that I seldom think a clear thought. They are all speckled with lightning flashes and whispering voices and feet going down long empty hallways and slow motion memories. I hardly slept last night. I remember how my grandmother smelled when she was dying. I will NEVER forget the sweetness of her breath and the scent of her hair as I bent over to kiss her forehead.

My period is a riot this month. I just sneezed and blew my tampon halfway out...excuse me while I fix myself up... Oh, the fun of womanhood.

It is hard being a person; becoming one is even more difficult. To be alone is the only thing that lets you see who you are. Aloneness will unlock the secrets inside of you. Be alone for a small part of your day and take a look into your heart.

jann

Words
June 18, 2003

Sometimes words tangle up your heart. They can mean so much and on the other hand, mean so very little. You must take good care with a word. It is so big and it goes out so far, that it would burst your heart if you really knew. A word can kill a soul. Steal a breath. Beat one down into nothingness. A word can lift. A word can liberate. A word can console. A word can heal and forgive and triumph over hatred. Words are the biggest things we have. They are all we have. It is the word that makes us human.

Words document who we were and are, where we came from and where we are going. These words define me. They show you who I am. They tell you my tale. Words are my past, my memories, my swords, my honour and my failures. I cling to your words. I hold them up to the light and look through them like stars. I read them over and over again. So few, but so many. I read under them and over them and between them. I look for crumbs inside the "Os" and the "As". I find so many things within your words to me. I find comfort mostly. Silence and stillness. I do not move when I read what you write. I sit and I stare and drink them in like an ocean. The salt must make an ocean endlessly thirsty.

Words make me thirsty for more words. Your words are like candy. Your words are like Jesus standing on a hillside with the sun on all those faces hoping that he really knows what he's talking about. Your words are songs and poems. They travel through space to find me here, sitting, looking out at my lake. I am holding them in my hands and they are like water. You cannot hold water in your hands for long; it seeps through onto the ground. And you watch it fall. And you see it drink in the earth. And that's how big a word is.

The word is everything. Humans are millions of tiny words strewn together with hope and love. I look at your words for hours and I repeat them in my heart. And I hold them close to my body like a shield so that no one can bring harm to me. The sky is blue and clear and for once so am I.

jann

Bursting In Air
July 6, 2003

I am in South Carolina. I haven't written, solely because I have been as busy as a whore on twin beds, end of story. I think it's been two weeks, but who's counting? Between the gigs and working on the documentary we shot in New York and my house and my family and my life, I have not had a moment to gather my thoughts long enough to write them down. I spent yesterday reading fan mail and once again was entertained, delighted, moved to tears, shocked, touched. I could go on and on... I won't. I am down here visiting friends for a few days before heading up to Toronto to shoot a video for the new single, "Love Is The Only Soldier." I feel like I haven't made a video in a very long, long time.

We ended up at a beach yesterday somewhere near Charleston. I can conservatively say that there were 100,000 people lining the shoreline that went as far as you can see in either direction. The Fourth of July weekend is crazy down here in South Carolina, USA. Firecrackers burst all through the night and I mean all through the night.

You can buy firecrackers everywhere. The signs say you have to be 18, but hey, we always managed to buy beer when we were 15 and 16. There was always some sorry soul who'd go in there and buy us a case of Extra Old Stock. What horrid beer that was. My mother drinks NO NAME beer. She says you wouldn't know the difference. I beg to differ. My mother also drinks COUGAR beer. She says sometimes it's cheaper than the NO NAME. Now that's funny.

I have to say, it's so fun lurching around and not having a single soul look twice at me. No hat, no glasses, no sheepish darts out to my car when too many people start following me through Winners...I feel like not shaving my armpits and wearing no bra.

jann

Winds Of Change
July 14, 2003

The wind blew my bedroom curtain sideways most of the night. It was nice for an hour or two and then just plain maddening. The wind is still thrashing about out there. My lilies are bent over like an old maid on a first date (I have no idea what that means).

The world is so strange. I cannot understand a single thing it does. I get up and try to just be what it is that I am. If only I knew. What defines me? I get so caught up in the record business. It has been my life for over 25 years. I think some days that I have forgotten how to live normally, whatever the hell that means. But then I think that I am SO normal, that it's affected how far I've gotten. I need to sleep. I sound like a loony tune.

Sweet Pea is sleeping with her head in her hands. She's holding her own head. I need to hold my own head. If my life were a single picture, it would be the one of me holding my first puppy. I am 9 years old with a black and white checked T-shirt on. I am squinting into the sun and I will never die.

j

Just A Moment
July 27, 2003

There is a sadness that has a hold of me today. It hangs on the tip of my heart by a jagged little barb. You cannot pull it out for fear of doing more damage. Life can eat you up some days and spit you out and swallow you whole.

ja

Good Deal
July 29, 2003

I feel better today. A game of golf and a bonkers Hollywood movie can cheer a girl up. I watered my thirsty plants. Saw Shrodie leap off the deck. I swear I am going to make him a cape with a big red "S" on it. He deserves some superhero type of costume. Anybody want to buy my house??? I'll cook you dinner. Only $9—worth every last cent if you ask me. It'll come with the cats. The word "assume" is ASS U ME. Think about that for a moment. Makes a whole lot of sense. Okay, it's time to stop writing, as I am apparently drifting into unconsciousness.

jann

Astonishing
August 3, 2003

Where did the week go? Behind me I suspect, through me, over me, under me and most certainly, into me. It has gone everywhere. I can see a dozen or so bees outside the window, hovering about the purple flowers. I don't know what they are called. What's new? They are tall and purple and lovely. What's more to know?

My trip to Toronto for the SARS/Stones extravaganza was quite simply astonishing. I have never, nor will I ever, see that many people in one place again (perhaps Winners on a half-off sale). We only found out about singing the anthem on Monday, so on Tuesday Nikki and I hopped on a plane and flew to Toronto. I looked at the clock when I fell into bed and it was midnight. A car picked us up at 9 a.m. and took us to a train, which in turn took us to a bus which then scuttled us to the back of the stage. We drove through people for 15 minutes...my mouth hung open like a hungry bird waiting for a big ol' worm watching them all trickle by us. They looked up at the bus and waved and cheered, not having a clue as to who was inside the thing.

It happened in a flash and was over even quicker than that. The masses. The humanity. It was wonderful having a half million folks or so singing the national anthem with me—and yes, I did know the words. I should have learned a line or two in French, but I didn't want to butcher what is otherwise a beautiful language...I figured I would just leave that to the pros.

It was a great day. The audience was so happy to be there. The sun was so hot. The 1/2-mile row of BBQs was something to behold. Whole sides of beef spinning around on a huge charcoal grill. The smell of onions and hotdogs and armpits and sun block and good old excitement lingered on everything

I wore as the police car (yes the police car) drove us to the airport, sirens and all. Thanks Sergeant Gary...that was the ride of a lifetime. Niks and I missed the 3:30 bus to get to the train to get to the cab to get to the airport, so Mr. Gary policeman drove us in his car at stock car speed. Well, it wasn't that fast, but the sirens were really cool. I made Nikki sit in the back so I didn't look as though I had been arrested.

The record is out on the 9th of September, so I am hoping for the best. The video turned out well. God only knows what the thing means. I am sure my mother will ask me what the story is, as usual... Believe it or not, I am going to meet her at Winners in 15 minutes. I need socks...

Started a cleanse, need to be near a working toilet...not necessarily in that order. Be careful with fibre.

jann

Going On
August 11, 2003

The jet plane is an amazing thing. I am sitting here, on a beautiful cedar deck overlooking Halifax harbour. Last night I played with the Dixie Chicks in Hamilton. There are tugboats steaming past me, pulling big ships full of grain or oil or sulphur or whatever it is that big ships carry inside of them. It is a still evening. My friend and I just went for a run around some little lake that had rowing races going on on it all afternoon (going on on it... sounds ridiculous). I have my feet up and it's lovely. Just this tiny breeze finding its way under my wet shirt is enough to make me not want to ever get out of this chair.

I can see the Citadel with its stone walls from here. I can see church steeples and the Halifax casino. Good combination. I can hear fog horns floating over the water. I can see sailboats and seagulls and the suspension bridge that runs from Dartmouth over to the big city. They tell me it's cheaper to live in Dartmouth. I am sure it is. The rows of houses here look like a postcard. The flowers are in full bloom. The lawns are all green and neatly trimmed, the shrubs kept and the sidewalks swept and the concrete steps proudly showing off their potted sunflowers. The jet plane; you can be anywhere in two days, anywhere in the world. You are a world away, it seems.

I am here for a few days and then back to Alberta to do the last two Dixie shows. So far, they have gone well. We haven't had things thrown at our heads or signs that read, "Get off the stage you nitwit." So, I guess it's all good. People have been good to us, loud cheers and warm applause and moments of quiet attention. I am grateful for that. It's exciting playing the big halls, the enormous stages and the hundreds of lights and the mass of people whose screams sound much like a freight train. There are times when I want to plug my ears. The first night in Toronto, I thought I would faint. I could not for the life of me catch my breath. I tried to suck in these deep, reviving breaths, but they stopped somewhere short of my lungs. Nerves I suppose. By the time you have yourself gathered up, it's over. Isn't that just how life goes?

jann

Got A Light?
August 15, 2003

It's good to be home, albeit for a short few days. I get rest-less here anyway. I am home for 3 or 4 days and then the rov-ing sets in. The Dixie Chicks' tour was fun. It's such a big, bold, blazing, out-loud show. So much to take in. They put on an excellent spectacle. Such great musicians. Great har-monies. The whole thing runs like a train on time. I enjoyed meeting them and thought the crowds were very kind to us. Being an opening act (which I haven't been in years) can be daunting, to say the least. But this was actually fun for us. No fuss. We played 40ty minutes and then sat back and enjoyed somebody else working their butts off. Their crew was respectful and helpful. Everyone was nice. You can't beat that. And they paid us...did I mention that? Weird, eh?

jann

You Are What You Are
August 22, 2003

I saw the video for "Love Is the Only Soldier" for the first time today on TV. My brother told me he had seen it in jail a few times and that he really liked it. He said if he hadn't seen my face, he wouldn't have known it was me. He told me that I was singing so differently. I told him it would only be temporary. It's just for one song I said, the rest I sing pretty much the way I always sing. He seemed concerned that I had changed my style. I didn't know I had a style.

Kathy Bates is one sexy motherfucker...

j

Perfect White Clouds
August 23, 2003

I flew over the big fire by Kelowna the other evening. The pilot came on and said that we should look out on the left hand side of the plane and see what indeed looked like the world ending. It was so beautiful. The smoke made a cloud so white and perfect that there are no words to describe it. There were "Oooohs" and "Ahs" and a lot of "Oh MY GODS"...The woman beside me said how terrible it was and I said that I thought it was beautiful somehow—she may have wanted to hit me...it was though. It was nature showing us how little we are. How little we always will be. We do not control the earth. It controls us. The universe can pick us up whenever it likes and throw us unto the abyss at its leisure.

j

So Much
August 26, 2003

We come squeezing into the world, covered with blood and gasping for our first breath of air. It is astonishing to me; the fact that we grow inside our mother's bodies for 10 months and then wait anxiously to be shown the light of day. It must hurt coming here. It must be terrible. I watched maternity shows yesterday and pretty much cried at every birth. The little fingers and toes and noses and cone-shaped heads yelling at the top of their little lungs. So much love...

The blinking, black eyes trying to figure out where in heaven's name they have landed. The "forget" switch that has to be turned on so they don't remember where indeed it was that they came from. God becomes a memory we have to relearn. So much love...

We try so hard. We don't control anything. When you surrender, you're much better off. My friend told me today that when she lost her mind, she found peace. I think I know what she means. I told her that I would like to lose my mind. She seemed to think that was funny. My mother told me that she was disappointed that I would never have grandchildren. It broke my heart. I heard it go "ping." Her words are stuck in my throat.

A butterfly just floated past...it is yellow and smiling, if that's at all possible.

j

You Know?
August 27, 2003

It's raining and I find it comforting. It's pouring down like a heartbroken teenager...I love a good, corny metaphor.

My parents had their 45th wedding anniversary on the 16th of this month. We all forgot—them included. My sister-in-law walked over to their house that morning and handed my mother a card. "What's this?" my mother inquired. "It's your anniversary, isn't it Joan?" said my sister-in-law. And that's the truth. 45 years and that's what it comes down to. My mother then phoned me and said that I had forgotten their anniversary. I rebutted by saying, "Ya, but you did too." I don't know if that makes us even or not.

j

Beginning Again

August 31, 2003

Russ's mother and my parents' best friend, Al, got married last night. My mother introduced them almost two years ago. Al's wife passed away from cancer almost 4 years ago as did Russell's dad 10 years before that...asbestos, the breath of death. It was such a great wedding. Julia (Rusty's mom) looked so radiant.

I met some Aussies on a plane last week and they wondered if it was pollution they were seeing out the windows... "God NO!" I said. "It's the fumes from the cow shit!!" (I actually never said that). They were coming to Banff and Lake Louise to do a travel show for their homeland. I told them every bit of useless information that I could. Their show is called "Destinations." They were such nice guys. All a bit perplexed by Clamato juice as well. Can't say as I blame them.

My dad has kidney stones that he thought was cancer. He was about to give us the combination for the safe in the basement...no such luck. Hopefully my parents will spend every dime of my inheritance if I'm lucky. I really hope they do.

jann

First Day is a Doozie
September 9, 2003

The new record, *Love Is the Only Soldier,* comes out today. I am relieved. We are all proud of it, a lot of waiting and a lot of working towards some kind of invisible thing. You can't see it, but you can feel it inside of you like a baby. There it is. Just like that.

The film fest has speckled Toronto with an eerie kind of glamour...a sad kind of glamour. It's hard to explain the desperation of it all. A "LOOK AT ME" kind of deal. Sell, sell ,sell. Exactly what I am doing these days and it makes me want to jump in front of traffic. A necessary evil, I'm afraid. Thankfully, the "look at me" stuff is short lasting and I will be back at Costco before you know it.

The record comes out today and I shall stand tall and try not to pay much heed to the nay-sayers. It's hard writing music that everybody likes. It's hard enough to write things that even I like. I thank you all for giving me the life that I have and I hope in some small way, I can contribute to your lives. God knows I try.

jann

Wondering Why
September 12, 2003

I watched a pregnant girl cross the street yesterday, barefoot, smoking, kicking at a paper cup. I watched her cross in a zigzag, through traffic to the sidewalk, where she then perched herself against a light pole. Just behind the smoking girl, leaning over her new baby in a beautiful silver carriage, was a neatly dressed young woman. The contrast took my breath and threw it on the floor.

The barefoot girl dragged away at her cigarette and looked off into the nothing that was her life. The new mother tucked a blanket around her baby and stared into the sun, squinting and waving at someone she knew. I pictured the unborn child inside of that little girl surrounded by God, still, somehow...loved. I heard the saddest song in my heart and I knew how important sorrow really was for me at that moment. Two lives intersecting and brushing past each other, as I watched from the window of a lovely hotel room, waiting for an interviewer to ask me why my music was so sad.

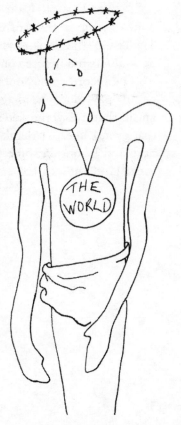

j

Thanks For Calling—Part I
September 18, 2003

A young girl came up to me on the street today, introduced herself and then bent over to kiss my hand. I didn't know what to say really. Thank you was all that seemed to come out of my mouth. A total stranger kissing your hand in the middle of the afternoon; magical somehow. Her face lit up and so did mine. I'll never get over all of this. Never.

j

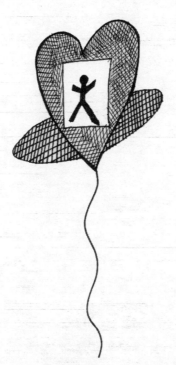

Thanks For Calling—Part II
September 18, 2003

How does one explain a song? Isn't the song supposed to explain the song? It's like describing the colour orange. How do you do that? You just compare it to other things and hope that people make a connection.

j

Taking The Plunge
September 29, 2003

I am sitting and looking out the window for the first time in nearly a month. I feel like a stranger in my own house, for a lot of reasons I suppose; the fact that I am never here and the fact that my heart has kind of moved out already. I have been folding laundry it seems, for 5 straight days. I have 65 pairs of underpants. I actually took them out of this disaster I call a "Panty Drawer" and counted them. I threw away 21 pairs of underpants as they were either missing their crotch or had somehow been used to clean up a crime scene at some point in their lengthy history. Good God Gordon is all I can say about that. I have such a sense of accomplishment! A drawer that I know the contents of! Shrodie is out. He snored all night. I changed the sheets and took off the feather bed I had on there, as I think it's breaking my back. I'll put it on one of the guest beds and let my company have a shit sleep (I didn't mean that).

I just want to say, get out there and plunge into your own little life. Do something you think you cannot do or think you do not like. There.

Everything has turned yellow and red and brown here this past month (including my underpants apparently). It looks breathtaking. I went golfing with some friends on Saturday and we all kept remarking how unbelievably beautiful it looked. We were happy to just stand there and look out into the hills. They were living art. They were so deeply looking back at us. Very weird. Fall always pulls me back 30 years to piles of leaves and rakes and turd fights with Leonard and Dale; Cheese Whiz sandwiches and grape Kool-Aid and S&V chips. We'd actually open the bag and count the chips out to each other, one by one, so it was fair. We went so far as to split them into piles of small, medium, large, and yes...burnt. We were nuts.

My parents, speaking of nuts, bought a pellet gun to shoot at the "mean squirrel." Apparently there are "nice squirrels" and "mean squirrels." They already own a bb gun, but that would kill the mean squirrel, says my father. I am not kidding. Mom said that the pistol only shot plastic pellets that would only scare the mean squirrel away. They have had a little red squirrel living in their woodpile for years and that is the one they are trying to help. The big mean squirrel chases her and her babies around and eats her food. Hey, that deserves a shot in the ass if you ask me. I can just picture my mother aiming a gun and firing it into a squirrel's ass. Jesus. Anyhow, if I write down the word squirrel, or the word apparently, one more time, I may have to kill myself.

I wonder if that barefoot, pregnant girl had the baby? Do you ever wonder about things like that? Do you ever walk by someone and say to yourself that you will never see that person again? I do. I do it all the time.

Saw Duray yesterday. He seemed unusually good. He has a woman back in his life from years ago and I think it's really making a difference. It's actually his wife...long story, but hopefully one that will have a happier ending than the last ending. Good English, eh? We played Scrabble and ate popcorn and drank pop. He started running and has lost 25 lbs. He looks so good. Better than he has in years.

Well, that's it for today. The world is unfolding. Go plunge into your life. Make it bigger than it was today.

j

Did Not
October 1, 2003

I have plenty of clean underpants to choose from today. Some I have never seen before. I should be concerned about that, but I am not.

jann

Older Than Me
October 11, 2003

I sat beside an old woman on the plane yesterday. I was in the window seat, 13A. I had to ask her to move so I could sneak in there. It was difficult for her to get up. Her every tiny movement was slow and deliberate and well thought out. It took her legs and arms and hands several moments to hear the message from her failing brain. A body is a jail cell of sorts. She asked me if I was alone and I told her yes I was. She hung heavily to the back of her seat while I made my way past her.

The people behind me were annoyed and in a hurry to sit down and wait. There were long strained sighs overheard...and a few "come ons" and the like, all cleverly mumbled under the sound of the plane's engines and the safety announcements. I got into my seat and said thank you. She laboriously sat down again and proceeded to situate herself comfortably—if that was even possible. She looked ninety-nine to me, although life being as hard as it is for some, it could have had her in her late seventies as well. Who knows these days? Her nails were lovely, bright reddish brown, perfect in every way. She asked for tea, milk and sugar; I had ice water and read the paper. She looked past me out the window a lot. I kept looking out there as well, perhaps trying to see what she saw. See-saw.

She took a bag of chips and a package of Clodhoppers off the snack tray. I declined. I watched her try and open the chips for what seemed to be an eternity. I didn't offer my help because I was somewhat torn; I didn't want her to feel helpless. I learned early on in my life that one should be careful when offering charity to the able. It can be offensive. The flight attendant finally intervened and all was well. And then the woman was on to the Clodhoppers and to the same recurring problem; the inability to open the package. I, once again, watched her fumble with the plastic edges, pulling and prodding and ending up luckless. I was just about to lean in and rip the package from limb to limb when the flight attendant came by to intercept my aid. I felt bad that I didn't offer help right away, but I still think it was her right—her dignified right—to do it for herself. She's older than me. She knows more. She's lived more and seen more and done more than I have and perhaps than I will ever do. I don't know what her life has been.

She had a tiny little clip in her grey hair. It held the coiled salt and pepper locks neatly behind her ear. She touched the clip from time to time to see if it was still there. I wondered who she was going to see, or if she lived in Calgary. I'll never know. I should have asked. I should have talked to her. I didn't.

She had her earphones plugged into the wrong hole the entire trip. She didn't seem to mind. She watched the news anyway. She kept fumbling with the volume and the channel changer; I never did a thing. I sat there, frozen; me the lump. I pictured myself old and alone on a plane and wanted to bawl. I saw myself as she was, trying to work things and trying not to be noticed because I could not do it for myself. Trying to open a bag of chips. Trying to pour cream into my tea.

The things I want are unknown to me. I don't know what I want. I just know that I feel empty some days and full on others. I think of Danielle, my friend with CF, and what she has endured. What she continues to endure with lungs in her body that once belonged to someone else. How can that be? I think about dying because it is a part of living. To ignore it is a tragedy. To push it away from ourselves is a dangerous proposition. I don't know why fully but dangerous indeed. There is a pain in being old, a triumph, a victory, a sadness. It is everything a human has ever felt in her lifetime. It is every day and every tear and every hearty laugh. It is every kiss and every touch and every disappointment. Oh, to be old and surrender it all. To not worry about love anymore, who loves you and who does not. To just lie there and feel content.

The old woman on the plane beside me looked anything but content and that broke my heart into jagged little bits. It bothers me still today, as I look out at all the fallen leaves, the gunmetal sky, the dark, cold lake. I watch your fish tank at the foot of your bed. The neon light. I listen to the water bubble away and the orange little fish darting about alone in there with no partner, no other.

Home again I am. Home is where I am and not where I live, I am discovering. I unpack my things for the millionth time and lie in bed and think about everything I've seen and felt and heard throughout the day. It's all too much. I hope somewhere, somehow, someone is getting it all down and remembering who I am and where it is that I am supposed to be going, because I definitely do not know.

jann

Thankful
October 14, 2003

I am thankful for everything.
I am thankful for a world that always brings sorrow and joy
and bitterness and bliss.
Thankful for the friends that have lifted me up and let me
down and straightened me out and let me fail. They are my
heart. They are my life.
I am thankful for my mother who stands up to the universe.
For my father who shows me how fragile and strong we can be
all at once.
I am thankful for lovers who have come and gone and given
me food for my soul and memories for my body.
I am thankful for the drunken night I returned home with one
shoe. I returned home...
I am thankful for my country and my countrymen and the
earth beneath my feet.
I am thankful for my house and my car and my cats that shit
and puke and sleep around my head at night.
I am thankful and grateful for the 3 wonderful people who
work for me and look after me and guide me and who get me
from here to there.
I am thankful for the music that keeps me from literally dying
and fading and disappearing from the world.
I am thankful for this mysterious process called living.
I am thankful that I don't wonder about it every second.
I am thankful for my brothers and my nephews. The diversi-
ty they show me everyday. Their differences that make them
just so. Their love for me.
I am thankful for my every breath. For breathing deeply and
feeling the life pound through my veins.
I am thankful for those who have more than me and regretful
for those who have not as much. I wish it were different.

I am thankful for peace and hateful of war.

I am thankful for the stars at night and for the sun in the morning and the dreams that make me want to try harder.

I am thankful for you. The shadow you are. The distance you are. The space between us. The wanting of everything else.

I am thankful for the lessons that pour though my hands like I am holding water...always making room for more.

I am thankful for almighty God; for the wondrous Goddess and for the angels and the wishes and the prayers that are always answered whether I know it or not.

I am thankful for all that I am and all that I will be.

I am thankful for every moment that I am here, drinking in the bounty of this endless love; the love that reaches into me and holds me up. The love I give that was never mine to keep.

Oh, this tiny world. This pained and glorious place we call home. May we all find what we seek and may heaven truly be a gathering place for forgiveness and new beginnings. Keep trying. Keep going, at all costs, never stop. You have the right to be happy.

jann

And Again
October 16, 2003

We are hard on ourselves. God whispers instructions, but we can't hear them because we are determined to figure it out all by our lonesome. We are so stupid and so lovable all at once. It is hard being a person. It is hard wondering about what will happen to us all—and not harbour some kind of distant, but all too noticeable, fear. Having said that, you certainly have to laugh at what foolish hearts we are. We are more bendable than breakable thankfully. We crash, but don't often start on fire...you'd think with all this fat we'd be able to fry up breakfast on our asses. We get winded, but at least we stop talking long enough to hear someone else. We are anxious, but not in a hurry to make it go away; sometimes it's better than feeling nothing at all.

God must be exhausted. I picture her there, on her cloud, looking down with head shaking side to side, a long sigh seeping out through pursed lips. I know how hard it must be to be God. No I don't. I don't have a clue. God is winging it...or is that the angels winging it? Winging...mine are all bent from picking my sorry ass up all these years. They are bruised and breathless and tired from me I am sure. I bet they laugh a lot.

Loving someone is letting them fuck up, no matter what the cost. I fuck up every single day and I don't know how else to begin trying to get it right without getting it wrong. If I am going to die, I am going to die trying, not waiting for something to happen, but actually be the centre of the happening itself. I sound like a fucking nutbar.

I often feel like I am in a circus and I am the high-dive girl who climbs up into the rafters of the circus tent, tipping my toes over the end of the wooden platform and preparing myself for a dive into a tiny bucket of water. It's a metal milking bucket with a wire handle and some rust around the edges.

I can hardly see it. It looks like a dime. The people are cheering in hushed frightened tones, waiting to see if I will jump and surely meet my end. I jump anyway, knowing that I am too big and that the water is too small.

I would rather that, than stand there and wait on that plank for life to pass me by. There will never be enough water to dive into. You just have to have faith that it's all an illusion anyway. Every time I jump, I take that plunge, the bucket gets so big and I get so small, that I end up laughing myself to sleep wondering what in hell's bells name I was so afraid of. You must always jump.

j

This I Know
October 24, 2003

At night when I lie there, eyes searching into darkness, looking at those floating shapes that keep you awake, I put my hands behind my head and thank God that I am here at all. I wonder how it all became and then I just go off and sleep and hope to wake up better than I was the day before.

Basically, you die every night and are reborn every day. You rest your body so that your soul can travel and relieve its burden for a few hours. It must be hard hauling this lard-ass around every waking moment; tiresome, laborious. A dream is a soul finally able to speak and it has so much to say that it's all quite confusing. "What the hell was that?" you find yourself asking. "It's a secret," says your soul.

I remember falling off a swing by my grandmother's house when I was very small. I had gone so high up, that my stomach would churn as I swept back towards the earth. I just simply fell backwards from the loss of gravity and hit the ground. I was on my back looking up at clouds and the metal chains swinging back and forth, now without their passenger. I stopped breathing because I could not for the life of me get any air in; winded as they say. Bloody horrible to do to one's self. You think this is it. This is what it must feel like to let go. Ever so slowly, your lungs become unstuck and you find relief in the form of air. There can never be enough air for me. I need a lot of it. My greatest of all fears is to not be able to breathe.

We all have to fall at some point...right?

jann

Have To Laugh
October 27, 2003

I will suffer knowing that I am from here, where no marks were made, where the cowboys bash around the gay boys and where hunting is the reigning sport of cowards. I will suffer knowing that Manhattan was never mine and that I never spoke Italian and that I never had sex with the good-looking men in Speedos with sand and hair and sweet wine pouring from my mouth. I am plain.

I will suffer knowing how little I was in light of it all. How small and insignificant I am among all these weightless beauties; that I am ugly somehow and that I have never been, nor ever will I be, a junky strung out, naked, wrapped around a toilet in LA somewhere, with my junky boyfriend. I will suffer in my romantic little head.

I will hear Rufus and know what shit I am. Not even a shadow cast by his sun. Not even that. Humility is a hard thing. You lie there looking about you as "they" walk over you without even so much as a glance down. They step over you at the party, wanting to surround themselves with the gorgeous, mindless, young things and the old men with money. I am so plain. I will suffer knowing that I was never smart or clever or pretty. You have to be one of those things in order to get into the party at all.

You have to laugh. It is the days when everything sweeps you away that you have to laugh your bloody little empty head off. Love is still bigger than me. It is still bigger and brighter and tougher than I will ever, ever be. Thank the angels and the arrows and the good Lord up above for love. I would never laugh again otherwise.

Rufus sings about love and you feel it pour out of you and into you in an instant. You smoke in the crystal meth with him and sit in the corner with a cigarette dangling from your dried up hungry mouth. His voice is endless and timeless and so painfully beautiful to listen to, that you want to sleep forever and then some. Rufus cries and you know that it was a deep and hopeless one...but he made it out despite everything. You have to fall apart and fall off and fall in. You might as well not be here at all otherwise. If you are not prepared to fuck everything up and at least try to live loudly and proudly and bravely, you WILL miss IT. I will suffer knowing how safe I always was and how afraid I was to confront anything or anyone; that I would just sit silently and let them all tell me who I was.

You have to laugh. If anyone knew where my body had been... Misery is such a simple state. It doesn't need explaining. You know it when you see it. You know when it is beside you, you can't miss it. It's heavier than the whole world. It's as heavy as humanity and all its cruelty. As dark as we are, this too is our brilliant lightness. As evil, we are kind and good. As hurtful, we are generous and forgiving. As sad, we are so

happy. We are quite something. I feel so good right now. Read past the words I write and you'll see it too.

When someone makes you cry so hard with their songs, that the snot bubbles out of your nose and you sit with your cats that are all wondering what in hell could possibly have gone so wrong. All the cats are wet with the tears of relief around this empty house today. When someone can show a piece of their world to you and say, "Here it is. It's so terribly frightening that you may just feel alright again when the song is done." Every night I die and every day I wake up and know that I can change anything I want to change. I don't have to stay in this place another moment. It's when you don't see the necessity—in that I fear for you all, as I would fear for myself. Change is the only hope we have.

Thank you Rufus, for all of your words; for walking the razor's edge and being able to tell us wee, plain people of your shattering, wondrous, miraculous travels.

jann

Mexicans With Lemon Tarts
October 28, 2003

A guy goes into the doctor's office, completely nude except that he is wrapped in Saran wrap. The waiting room is full of gawkers, jaw dropping stares and children's pointing fingers. The doctor ushers him into the examination room and begins his examination. "What is it, doctor?" says the man. "Well, I can clearly see you're nuts."

I thought I should start the day without the weight of the world dangling from my pen. It rained all day yesterday. Everything smelled so new and clean. It's odd seeing umbrellas unfold here. Does it rain that infrequently??? In Vancouver, you can buy an umbrella for 99 cents (they sell a lot of umbrellas). I have bought one of them on more than one occasion. I had this red and black umbrella in the back of my car for, I swear to you, years, when finally one day, during a sudden downpour, I said to myself proudly, "I can use that umbrella I have in the back of my car!"

I got out of the car, whirled around to the hatchback, pulled it out and opened it into the grey downpour. Well, my God, if I didn't almost get flown down the street like Mary fucking Poppins! The thing was huge!! I think I got it from some golf tournament...Anyway, it was so BIG, that I could barely fit down the street with anyone else. People looked at me with envy though, I could tell. It was the Hummer of all umbrellas. The Goliath. The Chrysler tower. It's still in the back of my car to this day.

I had a paper umbrella when I was a kid, with oriental pictures on it; little fans painted on with Geisha girls holding them in front of their faces. Every time I opened it up, it would stink so badly that my mother would comment, "Did you have that bloody umbrella opened up in here? It stinks." I like the word "umbrella." Sad when you can smell an umbrella. That can't be good.

Shrodie is sitting beside me waiting to be touched. He is my watchman. He loves to watch me type. He tries to type himself when I am away. I have found evidence:

Pppllea se HeelPP me.

I Em TRaappE d by a BiGG TTThhin Wit HHarre on IT. Cum N gitt me OuTTaa hare.

See what I mean?

It's cold in here today. I think I'll have to break down and turn the furnace on. It is, after all, the end of October. Halloween...my mom says that every year she sent one of us out as a Mexican, because she had a poncho and a sombrero... I think I was a Mexican a few times. Pat was usually the devil or one of the guys from KISS. Duray was a Mexican when I wasn't. Usually he'd go as a ghost. Just a sheet over his head with a few holes cut into it. Inventive. He was the guy egging everything and scaring the hell out of us at every dark alley.

The candy we'd come home with!! Tons, pillowcases full!! I am surprised I have a tooth in my head (I don't really...) There was always some urban legend afloat back then, about razor blades in apples or poison in the popcorn balls that the old lady in the corner house gave out every year. There was always a story about someone who actually died right here in boring old Calgary from choking on a caramel. Some kid would point and say, "It happened right there in front of Steve's house." Every year the tales were the same, only much longer winded and more outlandish.

It's good to be scared on Halloween. We never had safety issues in those days. There weren't reflective panels on our cat suits to alert the oncoming traffic. There weren't government standards set out as to how big the mouth holes in masks should be. We weren't all in fire retardant fabrics, or walking with a parent. I don't ever remember walking with a parent. How un-cool and un-scary is that? We took our chances. The world was different then. It was nicer somehow, kinder.

There were wars, but I don't remember watching them on TV. I loved Halloween.

When we moved out here at the end of the 60ties, Halloween took on a whole new meaning. This was farm country. The houses were a 1/4 mile walk in-between. No more running from house to house filling your pillowcases in mere moments, NO! Now it took hours of toil and strife and, God forbid, labour, to gather even a few morsels. And who would want their parents to drive even if they offered??? Not us. Not Leonard, Dale and I. We had our dogs and our pellet guns should anything go wrong. I am not kidding. There was always time to shoot at the odd stop sign on our travels for lemon tarts...yes, God damn lemon tarts!! Who gives out lemon tarts for Halloween? And where are you supposed to carry them? Idiots! We'd obviously eat them on the spot and give the crumbs to the dogs (it's very funny watching a dog chew gum. I highly recommend trying it out on your own). It must be hard being young these days, harder than it was for us.

It was so amazing coming home and dumping all my candy out on the bedroom floor; sorting through every piece and counting how many of everything you had. It was the most fun time. It was hard going to sleep that night. I'd keep one hand on the handle of my plastic pumpkin full of sweets and one eye open just in case anybody should pull a fast one. You dreamed candy. At school the next day, the kids would ask you what you got. You'd compare notes, you'd remark on where the best "candy houses" were. "What did you go as?" you'd ask. Funny, the passing of time. How we remember things. Our lives are memories strung together. Sometimes...just sometimes, they are little lights wrapped around our hearts.

jann

Freeze Freezing Frozen
October 30, 2003

The path to you is strewn with hanging things; vines with thorns and spider webs...
The path to you is delicate and complicated and precious and hard...
The path to you is intoxicating and luminous and blinding...
The path to you is not travelled enough to make the lines clear...
The path to you is a mystery and a riddle and a song...
The path to you is never the same way twice. Never the same one...

I don't know how to find the path, or perhaps I have been on it all the while. That is what is. The space we make in our hearts for another, remains empty long after they are gone.

The stillness of winter is lovely. The quiet hush of the cold. The faces looking out of the windows lit with candles and burning hearths. The geese that stop on the lake for a rest; I marvel at how their little webbed feet can stay warm beneath that black water. I envy them. To float without a care in the world—this or any other. To not fear whether or not a prayer has reached its destination. I envy many things about them.

I drove past 3 deer last night on my way to a friend's. I was on 101st Street heading north and there they were. Their delicate faces pulling up from the snow-covered grass, watching me approach in my car. I rolled the window down to get a better look at them and let the sheet of freezing air fall in. Big brown eyes and white tails and slender legs. I thought to myself, they survive out here all night long, on their own, knowing what to do. Watching out for each other. Jumping barbed wire fences and hiding from us all night long. That's why it's so nice to see them.

They followed me with their elegant heads and then they

were gone into the mist and the snow and the dark. It's so nice to see them standing there. It makes you feel like we may just make it after all—I don't know how, but somehow.

Mom and I visited Duray yesterday. The roads were so fucking terrible. We were an hour late for the visit. We played Scrabble and drank bad tea and ate the popcorn that he always brings into the visit. I hate it sometimes, going in there. Past the guards, through all the doors, down the gravel path onto the sidewalk, up the stairs, through some more doors, past some more guards, signing yet another sheet, a roll call if you will.

I hate it some days. I don't know how he does it. How he counts the time; that's all he does, is count the time. Mom and I talk about what we'll do when he gets out someday. Sometimes we don't say anything at all. Sometimes we just watch the fields blur past us; the hay bales and the clouds and the cows waiting for more of nothing. There is something about the prairies that is so comfortable and something that is so frustrating. I will suffer knowing that I am from here...and yet my gratitude is overflowing. It's all too much right now.

j

The Pain of Too Much Tenderness
November 3, 2003

I think the hardest part about love, or understanding it at least, is that you have to love someone and not expect to be loved back. It has to be given without ANY expectations. Love is just that simple. It struck me like a hammer late last night while I was reading *The Prophet* by Kahlil Gibran with a friend of mine. It is a wonderful book and it takes very little time, but much thought, to get through. "Love has no other desire but to fulfill itself," he writes. My favourite line so far is, "To know the pain of too much tenderness"... "To be wounded by your own understanding of love." I needed to be reminded of the painful beauty involved with loving anyone; especially yourself. When you are at your emptiest moment, so can you be totally filled with love; every available space in your heart, flooded with hope and joy and promise. We fill, we empty and so it goes, this life of ours.

I love many people, to each of them a part of me given unto no one else but them. If I love a hundred people, so it is that I am a hundred different versions of myself. I love no one the same. It has taught me how bendable love is, how pliable and moveable and changeable. When I have lost love so completely that I break apart, so it is that I rediscover the radiance of finding it again, or perhaps, it is love that finds me. I have felt unloved in my short life. We all have. I have felt the isolation of being left and I too have been the "leaver." I don't know which is worse. It is difficult leaving anyone behind you; closing a door and shutting it and leaving them forever. To walk away from someone you more than likely love still, but for whatever reason cannot be with them presently, physically, emotionally, soulfully. You become a version of yourself less than whole, less than wonderful, less than extraordinary. The days pour out so quickly onto the ground that you have to make sure that your adventure is nothing short of miraculous.

We all need to be with someone who makes us feel like we can do anything. If you are with someone, be it a lover or a friend or a sister or a brother, that makes you feel anything less than inspired, you may want to rethink that connection and how much time you want to spend "trying" to make it work. Walking away means that you are walking towards something too. Be inspired. Be motivated. Be with someone who respects your thoughts and your heart and your person. Be happy at any cost. By that I mean, making changes and moving forward without even a glance behind you.

Life is such a state of mind, you cannot for a second think that things will just right themselves. You have to be involved in what happens to you. I often hear people say, "Well, it's up to God now..." Good Lord, if it were up to God, I think the planet would be vacant, or we'd all be back in training camp somewhere up in the clouds with a teacher saying, "Oh my, I don't know if they'll ever be ready Jesus. All they do is fight, kill, ruin, conquer and eat." Half the fun of going to IKEA is that you have to build the shit yourself. "Here's your shelf, now go build the thing." The satisfaction of actually doing something for yourself, that's how God works too. "Here's your life, now go and build it." I like that.

I know you can't always love your life; it's hard some days and easy others. The thread that holds it all together is more like a hair right now, so fine and fragile. The bad makes the good seem so much sweeter though. On my worst days, I say to myself, "the good will be even better this time around." You have to believe that there is a balance and a purpose and that you being here at all is deliberate. I am glad that you are here. The world is better with you in it. Love is such a little word and it's bigger than anything I have ever seen or felt or known. All my cracks, all my fractures...this is where the light indeed comes pouring in. If I were perfect, how dark my house would be. I would have no place for mercy or forgiveness to writhe itself in through. I love all my cracks—suddenly that doesn't sound all that poetic...

j

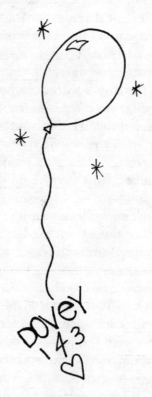

The Merit O fVaseline (PG)
November 7, 2003

My dad's blood pressure was over 200 today. It has been for the past few days. I fear he may explode. My mother's blood pressure is fine. She thinks dad's may be high because he checks it all the time. You know, when you're expecting it to be high, it's high. Mind versus matter type of deal. My blood pressure is unknown at this particular moment. I think I am alive, but as Russell said to me yesterday while eating Vietnamese soup, "How do we know we're even here?"

It is clear and blue and bright here today. Not one single hint of a cloud, not a wisp, not a thread. It is just perfect. Shrodie didn't last long out on the stoop. He doesn't like his feet to get wet and the snow is melting. One of the cats (Maybe I am sure), has puked out something that may have been a hair/food combination. It is horrific. I was shocked as I came down the stairs to work. It was shit brindle brown and approximately 15 inches long. I am going to leave it for a few hours so that it dries somewhat and so that I don't dry heave too badly while scooping it up. Honestly, I don't know what to do. My mother swears by Vaseline. She puts it on their paws every time she comes down to feed them when I am away. "Just put it on their paws Jann and they won't get hair balls," she says. "They love it." Who wouldn't? I often find myself staring into the Vaseline jar with a piece of dry toast in my hand, pondering endlessly...

My gram used Vaseline on her face for 75 years or so. She looked angelic. My mother uses it all over her body every time she gets out of the bath. How do you pull up your pants with that stuff on? I'd need to lie down with pliers and tongs and God knows what else. She has a giant tub of Vaseline in every bathroom in their house. In fact, I don't even think it's the "Vaseline" brand, but a cheap generic imitation. What in heaven's name is it made of? I think you'd be better off smearing Cheeze Whiz all over your ass. That's where it ends up anyway, am I right???

My dad has put "Vicks" in his nose every night of his life. I'd put my life on it that he has a jar by the nightstand right now. He also has a box of Kleenex and about 5 pocketbooks that he'll read in a matter of moments. My mother has an extra pair of glasses, Avon hand cream and a stack of magazines from June of 1978. I'd put my life on that too. I have a clock radio, 20ty or so hardcover books, hair elastics, a water glass, chewed gum, a candle and a flashlight. I also have a large walking stick with a bell on the end of it that Dad made me; it's for killing (or maiming at least) burglars. I hope I never have to use it.

jann

A Good Look
November 12, 2003

Life is remarkable. We don't think about it much; we just get up and eat toast, drink coffee and go to work worrying ourselves sick over what we're wearing and how our asses look. It's no small task getting a good look at your ass either. Health is all we really have. It is the centre of us. It is our lives. I have a friend in peril. It is heartbreak bigger than the sky when you cannot help someone to be well. It's like standing and watching a child drown. It's like watching a train full of doomed souls roll out of the station. Helplessness is not hopelessness though. There is something to be said for that. Hope sustains life; hopelessness causes death.

The litany of things that can go wrong with the human body is nothing short of astounding. Anything and everything can bring us to our knees. Yes, sometimes we are to blame for our own demise, but more often than not, sickness is random; it just picks on whomever it wants. People who have never smoked or drunk or eaten anything with a mother are not immune. No one is safe.

You can take every vitamin in the world and yet fall prey to MS or CF or TB or whatever. I always think to myself, "why not me?" while others are surely thinking, "Why me?" Goodness is not rewarded; evil is not punished. I ponder that lesson often. We all want so badly to live as long as we can. We want to keep standing up and facing it all. For a lot of people, it gets just too hard.

Schopenhauer, a German philosopher, once said, when people are more afraid of living than they are of dying, they will take their own lives. I can't fathom that kind of fear. I don't know it; I have never tasted it, although I have witnessed it. I have known three people that have taken themselves from here. I don't recommend doing that.

It is hard being sick. It picks away at you like a crow on a carcass. Maddening. Fearlessness is something I admire. My friend is fearless, even though she may not know it. She's in pain and yet she still laughs and still makes everybody around her laugh. She knows things about living I will never know. She is giving and complimentary and concerned about everyone else around her. She worries more about the struggle her family faces with her illness, than her own feelings. She is remarkable. She is extraordinary. She is steadfast and strong and hearty.

You don't know how strong you are until you are tested. We would rather not be tested but...I would rather not be tested, but somehow I am always grateful that I have been. I don't learn otherwise. I am grateful for my wellness. I am ashamed at my lack of acknowledging that more often, if not always.

I am proud of my friend and I am scared for her. I don't know how to help, what to say or do or feel. I'll just pray harder. I'll just keep hoping just like she does. Miracles are everywhere.

jann

Thirty-Four Long
November 13, 2003

Looking out of this window, you'd never know the world was falling apart. One almost feels guilty about the peaceful existence we enjoy here. The quiet is ample. The snow hasn't a single track in it. It is pristine in its stillness. I am living inside of a glorious book. The cats are on their chair; Shrodie's ass is covering Sweet Pea's face, Maybe is hiding. I have never seen a cat so typically afraid of everything. A "fraidy cat"...she is the low man down. She is the scapegoat for every pile of puke I find in this house. The other two cats point at Maybe and say, "It was her." I feel so bad about it.

I am hoping that Mom and Dad will take her in their new house. Mom is so good with her. She actually picks her up and is able to brush her. I can't do that very often. I have to track her for days with an Indian guide, then and only then, do we locate her in the lining underneath the leather couch in my office and I am not kidding. I see just the very tip of her jet black fuzzy tail dangling from the wooden struts and the frayed fabric. You'd miss it if you were to even blink. She is the Houdini of all cats. I should sell tickets. I got her when she was 3 months old and she has not changed a bit in 6 years. I spent most of the first year looking for her. She was hiding behind the dryer for two days one spring. She can't meow, so it's hard to find a mute cat. I should have called her Helen (that is a terrible joke, but funny nonetheless).

I cannot fathom anyone WANTING bigger boobs. Well, I suppose I could... I would have been a better volleyball player with smaller boobs, a better long-distance runner, a better pool player (you cannot have a boob plugging the side pocket all the time, now can you?)

Ahhh, the boob. The things it can sell: cars, hamburgers, jewellery, boots, Ski-Doos, trucks, men's cologne, underpants, hair products, gym equipment, gum, shoes, farm machinery, you name it, the boob will sell it for you. I am going to put boobs on my next CD cover. Maybe just one big old boob. In fact, I'll call the next record, *BOOB*.

j

In Your Eye
November 18, 2003

The rain makes people cry; all the wet faces, misted and shining and sad somehow. I was walking back to where I am staying umbrellaless and couldn't help but think how odd everything was. Rain slows things; footsteps hang in the air longer, everything is silent, just the humming of nothingness and the tears that make us all weak. I walked past at least a dozen people begging for change. I would have given one of the fellows money had he asked, but he didn't. Everybody else but he, did. I had my hand in my pocket, tightly bound around the edges of a loonie.

It doesn't bother me walking by them all the time, just some of the time. It bothers me most when I really SEE them. I don't often take the time to look into the person's eye; it is too hard on me. I feel a great sense of shame for just going past them like an emperor. I feel like if I don't look them in the eye, then I can save face and not feel anything. Pathetically it is the dogs nestled by their sides that make my heart ache the most. Their big black wet noses and their soaked mangled fur and the ropes around their necks. The sign more than often reads, "Need food for dog." The dogs don't know they're begging. They just love without any hesitation. It is painfully beautiful. God give me grace to know that kind of love and to give into it freely.

I wonder what happens to every single soul I pass? I think to myself, I will never see that person again. I am seeing them just this one time and then they're gone for good from my little life. A woman passed me on the street and mumbled my name. It was surreal. I turned back and tipped my head and said, "How are you?" She laughed. I thought that was a strange reaction to have. I didn't want to stop and talk. The rain was making the world blurry. I wanted to be alone in my head, hearing my name just snapped my dazed dream. Sometimes you just want to dream the whole world up.

The rain makes the colours bleed away down the drains. Trees barely cling to their green, the paved roads are mirrors and the headlights are blinking eyes. No one looked happy today as I walked past them. They had an element of blank. "Pain has an element of blank" wrote Emily D. How I love her words. The depth of her pain caused from simply living. People looked woeful and lost. Heads down and arms at their sides, counting lines in the sidewalk, careful not to step...and break your mother's back. Listen to the rain, hear it pitter-patter. Bones are dampened for days. A deep ache takes hold of old injuries. My hips feel my heart beating in them. I stood and held my face up to it, the rain that is, and let it pour down. I opened my mouth slightly and let the clouds fall in. I stared up for a long while and then carried on my way. Not knowing a soul that I passed. Not knowing anything at all really. Rain is the sorrow of a million broken hearts and broken hands; if I could simply wish all of that away from this place...

When Mom and I were driving home from an outing in town a few days ago, we witnessed a beautiful deer being struck by a speeding car just ahead of us. We watched the deer walk out to the highway and then bolt into the oncoming car. It was a woman driving. I looked at her out of my window as she passed, talking on her cell phone, heading somewhere very important. Our screaming began then, although we couldn't hear ourselves. It was in our lungs fighting to get out.

She smashed into the deer, severing one of its antlers off of his head. His body flew up and spun around a time and a half and then landed on its side. Bits of fur...air bound...black eyes shocked by it all. He was stunned I am sure, nearly to his death. I heard my mother scream my name. It was the worst sound I have ever heard in my life—to hear your mother scream your name in fear. The deer scrambled up and into the ditch. The woman in the car never stopped. She never fucking stopped. I have thought about that deer every day and hope he didn't suffer long. I don't know how anything could have lived through that.

j

What's Love Got To Do With It?

November 21, 2003

We don't know what we are looking for, we are just looking. We don't know what we want, we just know that we want something. One word, and only one word, can summon up so much of what it is that we do not know: love. The word that is whispered inside of our souls, that echoes in our dreams and our every waking second here on the earth.

I have stood in the airport so many times and just watched the goodbyes and the hellos and all the love that goes and comes with them. The leaned-forward bodies craning to see the last glimpse of the back of a head as it walks away, as it turns around the corner...and our waving hands that get caught, up in the air. A wave is the ultimate gesture. It is bigger than any motion we can make with our bodies. Bigger even than the blowing of a kiss. A wave can tell you so much about a person and about yourself. If only there were a wave "hello" to every wave "goodbye," but sadly there cannot be. People do finally leave us for good. Funny to say "for good." I hope it proves to be right.

I say goodbye too many times. I seem to be able to walk away from people and never look back. That makes me feel odd somehow. To perhaps not want to see myself turn into the biblical pillar of salt...or was it ash? To not want to look back, although I most certainly do, at least once, to make sure I am gone and that they are gone. When I look back at old relationships, I often wonder if they were even real. Were they ever in my life and was I ever in theirs? All I have is a few songs to remind me of a feeling—that's all. Love is what I honestly want to understand more than any other thing. It is why every word I write down seems so repetitive. I look at all the words written on all the pages and I pour over them, searching for some little thing I might have missed. What other kind of a song could there be, but a love song? What else could ever be as important as that? What?

I have moments when I feel so close and so free, but it would kill me to stay there. It would make me dissolve into thin air...the air that catches your hand as you wave goodbye and hello all at once. It's one of the first things we teach our children; to wave goodbye. We prepare them for the endless stream of them, "Wave goodbye baby" we say to them, "show them you can wave goodbye." And when they do finally, it is so adorable, perhaps because they don't quite know what it means yet.

I know that love is all of it. It is the whole of the universe and the whole of me. And if that love is only for a moment, then it is the moment I shall savour and take with me on my way. I will not remain bitter and hopeless, but rather I shall live with the bravery and the desire to march onward in search of something I may never ever find. I have made so many mistakes. I have been wrong so many times. I have lost so many things and people. But once in a while, God does grant me the serenity to let me feel something beyond my own humanity; the love that whispers inside of my soul, the love that says it is alright to not be perfect. I can live with that. I cannot live without it.

jann

Round And Round We Go

November 30, 2003

There is a mist hanging over the lake. I fully expect to see a ghost glide up to my window and peer inside at me sitting here. It's deathly quiet. I can hear the furnace kick on and off, seemingly confused at what temperature it wants to be. I can hear a clock ticking somewhere. The bird clock in the bathroom perhaps...no wait a minute, it's my watch. I hear my watch ticking. I seldom take my watch off. I feel odd without it. A habit, I suppose, that needs breaking. For some reason, I like to know what time it is. I don't NEED to know, I just like to know. Wow, what a startling revelation on this fine Sunday morning. Fuck am I boring.

I am not reading these days, which concerns me somewhat. I know it's not a time issue; more of a concentration issue. Maybe it's good to take a break from all the words. I have so many books I want to read. My nightstand is a mountain of ideas waiting to jump off the pages into my brain. My dad reads 3 or 4 pocketbooks a week. He is his mother. She kept reading, with just part of an eye, right to the end. Her glasses could have burned many an ant. I remember doing that with Leonard and Dale, burning ants with somebody's glasses, but they weren't ours. I also remember getting a wood burning set for Christmas one year. I loved that thing, dangerous as it was. I think I got in a fair amount of shit for burning bedroom walls and car doors...things like that. I burned the soles off of a pair of shoes one evening. That took some time.

Russell and his wife Barb had their baby. A little girl named Stella May Opus Broom. She is so cute. It's our first band baby. I figure I'll be the hairy old "aunt" that she will be afraid of someday. We all need one of those. I don't think I had a scary aunt; they were all pretty good actually. My dad's mother smelled a bit "off" near the end—and she cheated at cards—

but that was about it. My mom always talks about her eating over the sink, (my grandmother, not my mother). I wasn't as close to Grandma Richards as I was my mom's mom. That happens I suppose. My dad's mother's name was Crilla. She could be fun from time to time. She taught school for a hundred years, so she knew how to discipline the hell out of everybody. She was a big woman, had diabetes and never seemed to want to be here after Grandfather died. She said she wanted to go and be with him...love. She was a determined person.

What a time they lived in! She actually came up here with her family at the turn of the century, from Utah, in a covered wagon. Good God. My dad's side of the family were all good Mormon folk. Built the Cardston temple if you can believe that. I think we were stormin' Mormons...drinkers and smokers and bingo playing crazies. Dad talks about his dad having a beer behind the church in the 40ties. Who could blame him? 6 kids and two jobs and dead from a stroke at 56. Life can be so hard. You have to live it up once in a while. I never met that Granddad. Everybody talks about what a nice man he was, good-natured they always say. Good-natured? I like that. I figure I am pretty good-natured; maybe I got it from him.

My friend's grandmother is dying right now and it's so hard watching it unfold from afar. It makes me remember how difficult it was for my family when Gram decided to go. My Great-aunt Ern once told me that it wasn't easy to die. She said you can be as ready as you want to be, but it's still not easy. I remember being comforted somewhat by that and frightened all at once. When you lose a Grandmother, you lose a part of yourself you may not even have known you had. It's like you remember where you came from suddenly; that they were a portal for you to enter through into this life, this plane. It's supernatural and magnificent. Time becomes even more precious. You know that surrendering the idleness of youth is imminent.

The grace that the elderly give us; the stories and the lessons and the love. It's so big and so pure and so wonderful. It is simply hard saying goodbye to someone so dear. You can't seem to pour over the memories fast enough. You cram every conversation you ever had into your head at night and feel the tears roll onto your pillow. It feels lonely. You feel their pain. I am thinking of my friend's grandmother, wishing her good things on her way...grateful to her for your existence on this planet. My life is changed because of someone I will never know and who will never know me. And the circle is unbroken... "It is still a beautiful world, strive to be happy." And that we will.

jann

Choices— Part I
December 9, 2003

It's cold here today. It looks like a baking powder sky out there, the lightest mist floating down through the grey. The kids are skating out on the lake. I hope that it's good and frozen...God forbid somebody should fall though the ice and force me to call the fire department (I could throw them a cat.)

jann

Choices— Part II
December 9, 2003

Music is a wonder...it does things to us that we will never fully understand. It is a common language without colours or borders. ALL music is important and vital. One man's ceiling is another man's floor. I don't ever forget that.

jann

Cold Or Flu
December 11, 2003

I have been cold all day; can't seem to knock the chill out of my bones. I think finally, that that cold or flu (or whatever in hell it is) is coming to get me. I had one of those sleeps that are fitful, plugged up and restless. I guess fitful and restless are pretty much the same damn thing. My throat is at the beginning stages of soreness. Thank God really, because I should be getting sick now and not in six weeks. Being sick on the road is as much fun as a break-up. Maybe even more fun...

I don't feel all that much like celebrating anything...well, the fact that I am alive is always worth a fairly large Hurray! (I can't stop sneezing...to the point where it's hard to type). They, whoever that is, start Christmas so early that it's hard to get your nuts up when the time finally does come around. The whole thing "gets on my tits"—as my friend Nigel in London, England would say. I'll get cheerier no doubt after a couple of hot buttered rums...or is that runs? One goes hand in hand with the other when one is sick. You are afraid to fart, lest it be a Hershey squirt or something even worse, the dreaded "soft serve." Ah, humanity...add one week of bleeding, and voilà, you have perfection.

I should make some soup, but I am just not hungry. Have a thing I am committed to tonight. I should go...bit of make-up...lot of makeup...tons actually. The cats are all loopy, running about like they are in Siegfried and Roy. I know Shrodie would drag me to the neighbour's if I had a stroke...I just know it. See? A few laughs, a couple of spiritual ponderings and a bit of chicken soup for the soul. And I thought I had nothing to say???!!!!!

j

To Jann, From Kitty
December 18, 2003

I am feeling better than I was. Just stuffy (and that's just my personality). The snot is endless and my nose is starting to resemble Rudolf's. There was a large blob of cat puke at the top of the stairs that I stepped into this morning. It was still warm and wet and everything horrible. I screamed and then hopped into the laundry room. This blob actually managed to give me the dry heaves. I can usually scoop it up with 34 yards of paper towel and not even miss a beat, but this morning I couldn't manage to look at it without wanting to cry. I mean, what did this cat eat? It didn't look like anything I've fed them...it was bigger than a 44 ounce porterhouse steak.

I can't wait for the "Christmas" pukes to start happening. You know, when the tinsel starts coming out of their asses and they gag up pine needles and ribbon. The only problem with the pine needles is that I have a fake tree. What does that make my cats? Just so you know, Jesus was not born on the 25th of December...food for thought. It was a popular day for the Pagans, the solstice and all... Back to cat hurl...I would rather clean shit.

I have flooring in my living room that disguises the cat puke. Maybe I should change the flooring to something bright green or fuchsia that would at least let the stuff show up a little better. My mother said to me that I mustn't be putting Vaseline on their paws every day, because when she looks after them, there's no "throw-up" anywhere. I don't know what I am doing wrong. Is it wrong to feed them pot??? It's so funny for hours at a time (please know how much I am kidding...the fact that I have to even write that down is alarming. If you only knew the letters I get). I would like to have a dog. Maybe at the new house I'll go to the SPCA and get a dog.

Shrodie will have somebody new to beat up.

I am going to watch the news and see what's going on in this old world of ours. I have clean sheets on the bed. My phone is still connected. My parents are doing fine. I have friends that put up with me. I feel lucky to have what I have. I don't even mind having warm puke between my toes every now and again; it lets me know I am still doing fine.

jann

Will Sing For Food
December 22, 2003

    I had a really good sleep last night. I dreamt that I was backstage at some convention. I had on a black sequined shirt and pyjama bottoms. To top it off, I was trying to get into a bunk bed with some guy in overalls. Apparently I've got issues.

    I have to go grocery shopping today. I don't have a thing in this house. Well, I have a giant jar of Adam's peanut butter. You can only eat that for so long before you suck your own teeth out of your head. I have to figure out why I have been staring at a giant pile of laundry thinking it would fold itself. These cats are

useless...would it kill them to fold a T-shirt? I'm hungry.

NO running for me today. I am riding the white saddle and I don't feel like doing anything but eating. When you feel like spaghetti and meatballs at 9:30 in the morning, you know your hormones have derailed. I feel like opening a can of artichoke hearts...that can't be good either. Maybe a grilled cheese sandwich with pickles...maybe I'm pregnant? I think you need a drive-in for that. What I wouldn't do for Cheeze Whiz and celery...in fact, I think I may just have that.

I went to The Diner last night, as I haven't been there for a while. We have the cutest little hamburgers on the menu now. I guess they are mini-burgers. I saw a few platters of them go by and for a moment it made me think of "Whimpy" from Popeye. Remember him? Anyhow, they look really good... I see I am still on the food thing...

I should go get into the shower and get on with the day. I want to lie here with a heating pad and not move a muscle, but I'll do that in 46 years from now...if I make it that far.

j

Every Day
December 24, 2003

It doesn't feel much like the 24th of December. Where's the snow? But then again, who needs snow? Every year for the past 15 years or so, I've had a whack of my friends and family over to celebrate still being alive. Everybody eats shrimp and chicken skewers and candy and shortbread. We all drink mulled wine and whine about how quickly the year has gone by...again. We look at each other and say, are we really 41? Last year, it was, are we really 40ty? The year before it seems we were saying can you believe we're 30ty?!!!! Time has a way of slipping beneath our noses as we sleep. I am clinging to time. I am clinging to it and yet trying to release my grip long enough to look over the hills ahead of me. It's hard to see anything when you have your arms wrapped about the trunk of the tree...you have to go out on a limb, because that's where the fruit is.

The days of always looking behind me are becoming fewer. There is nothing there that I want anymore. Sure, there are memories that have made me and moulded me and scolded me and reminded me that going forward is the best possible path to take every time. I read a wonderful thing a few weeks ago and if I have written it here, I want to take this opportunity to write it again. Human beings have the wonderful gift of learning from their lives and experiences, and they also have the wondrous opportunity to forget and make more room for learning things. We all need to forget things. Old debts. Cruel lovers. Harsh words. Disappointments. Mistakes, oh the mistakes we make... We have to move ever forward, and for heaven's sake, we need to try not to look back over our shoulders. Like I always say as I head out of the door with my suitcases, what I've forgotten, I'll just get when I get there. Life is like that. I don't drive all the way home for a forgotten toothbrush anymore. Little things will bog you down. The world is grander than that.

I took my parents to *Lord Of The Rings, Return Of The King* yesterday and it was really quite lovely. They were so dressed up—to go to a movie??? They looked like they should've been on top of a wedding cake. They watched the movie intently, eating fistfuls of popcorn and drinking pop. I thought to myself, you won't forget this moment. It'll be there when I go, a white flash and a grin.

I am hanging on to their faces today still and in bed last night, going over their hands and their feet and their mouths. I don't know how else to explain it. They are so dear to me and I don't think, in fact I know, that I don't tell them how I feel...enough. It's hard to find the words. It takes courage. I don't have a lot of that. I am always so grumpy...always too many things on my mind. My parents...they are the door I came through.

This time of year always brings me to ponder deeply my older brother's life. It is terribly hard for him at Christmas because of the memories; ones he says he tries to wipe from his soul, but can't—the tree and the presents and the Rumoli games and my gram and the turkey and the green bean salad and the fruitcake and Dad's sugar cookies. He sits in his cell and wishes it all away. I am sure most of the guys do the same thing. Some, however, are still busy being evil; that's what's at the heart of who they are.

Apparently a couple of brainy inmates in Bowden took it upon themselves to piss into the broth my brother was going to make turkey soup from...gallons of it. The little stupid pricks figured they'd revel knowing that the warden would be eating it...my brother thought differently. He said something to the kitchen steward...about them pissing in the pot as it were. Now the little stupid pricks want to kill my brother.

They want to gather a throng of others and take him out. I also need to mention that the "soup" would have been fed to a hundred or so family members that were visiting their fellas for the Christmas social. My brother said he simply could not live with that and that he would have to say something, despite the fact that he knew he'd receive death threats. I also need to mention that my family was not there, so it wasn't us he was trying to save. I think that's important to note. I also need to mention that my brother has hundreds of grateful guys in there, whose families were spared a huge indignity. I believe they all stand with him against these foolish pranksters. "Prankster" seems too light of a word for the little shits. Anyway...

That is his Christmas. My brother is fair. He always has been, despite what others judge him to be. No one works harder than he does. He is someone you'd want on your side and the soup incident is a perfect example of that. He always stood up for Patrick and me. We never feared the long bus ride to school. We never had to. He was there. I wish his life were different. I hope he comes home some day, another year and another year and another year. It is hell for all of us.

I send good wishes out to everyone this Christmas. I say Christmas not to be politically insensitive, but rather because it's what I know. It's my heritage. I have nothing but respect and love for everyone and everything else that exists on this planet. I pray that we all find peace within ourselves and therefore, peace within others as well. I hope that we forgive our own shortcomings and that we can forgive those who share those same burdens. Every day, not just every new year, is an opportunity to start again. To be someone you want to be or know you can be, every day, not just the first of January. So many chances, not just one. People would have you think that chances run out; they don't. Be gentle with your soul.

Strive to be happy. A wise man once said, "It is still a beautiful world."

God bless you.

jann

On The Road Again
January 6, 2004

I am sitting here in front of the television. I haven't a clue as to what I have been watching. The tour bus is picking me up here, at home, around midnight. I shall be ready, in my pyjamas, suitcase in hand, slippers on my feet, ready for bed. I don't know if I have ever slept more than a few moments on the bus. I just can't seem to go to sleep and stay asleep. It is anything but glamorous. I mean, we have so much fun that it's a sin really, but sleeping in those tiny moving bunks is a bit of an artform. Russ sleeps like the living dead...in fact, most everyone else does. Maybe it's the princess in me...yeah, right.

We are off to Kelowna tonight, rehearsing a wee bit tomorrow (mostly technical stuff at this point), and getting ready for our first show on the 8th. I am very excited to get out there and play. It's such a rush to the soul.

It's colder than a witch's tit out there right now, colder than a shoulder, colder than a frying pan in the back of a pick-up truck, colder than a tongue stuck on an iron post. It's cold.

Sweet Pea is lying in front of the fireplace, licking whatever it is that she licks...her arse usually. I suppose if I could, I would. I don't know what else I have to do around here. I changed the sheets on the bed so I can hop into nice new clean ones when I am home here on the 22nd. It's always really weird playing at home. Too many people I know come to the shows. I look out into the audience and pretty much recognize everybody in the first 5 rows...and my parents always make me nervous, I don't know why. I have to really watch the swearing. Anyhow, here I sit, anxious and watching the time tick by. When you want it to linger it disappears and when you want it to pass, it hangs there like funeral. That's just the way it goes.

Well, time to relax a bit and check my luggage one last time. I bought the guys a bucket of KFC for the bus. It'll be gone by 5 a.m. I am sure. See you all out there. Thank you in advance for making my day.

j

Sleepless In...
January 20, 2004

I am in Grande Prairie. I slept until 12:32 p.m. according to the clock radio beside the bed. I had the world's worst sleep. To think I was in bed at 9 o'clock.

We are, as usual, having a great time. I laugh so hard every day that I am going to need Depends by the time my 42nd birthday rolls around. Lyle has been a complete ass...Russ has been doing some strange rock and roll God on stage during sound checks and that kills me as well. The guys are playing so fantastically. Every note so far has had me hanging in mid-air. Very pleasing and very easy to let yourself sink into another world on stage. The set list relies heavily on the new record, but we are all thrilled to be playing new songs...and old, so no fear.

My mom and dad are up here tonight so they are coming to the show with friends. I miss the cats. Janine is looking after them, as Joan and Derrel are here and not there. I'll see them in a few days, although I must tell you that it is hard going home for a night or two because it screws up my routine. It's almost better for me to go to a hotel. I just figure the cats get upset all over again. Nothing worse than those three little heads watching me pull out of the driveway again...they HATE the suitcases.

My dad would be saying, "Oh for Jesus Christ's sake Jann...those God damn cats don't know a God damn thing." He doesn't mean it though...all hot air at this point in his life. He bought a new blood pressure machine, at Costco no less. Maybe that'll cheer him up. He took my blood pressure on the old one he had and it was 200 over 160!!!! Fuck... He said to me, "I think you're gonna die." My mom said, "Oh for heaven's sake Derrel, take it again. That can't be right." No shit, I said.

Anyway, it feels good to be out here. I can't sleep on the

bus either, so I may be a zombie by the time we hit Toronto...make that Regina. Perhaps I need someone to make Velcro pyjamas; that would at least hold me steady in the bed as we took the corners at 5 in the morning.

I have been thinking about dying these past few days. Every now and again it seeps in and I think how very surreal life is, this dream that winds around a life. The real and the unreal of who we are and where we are and what we are. It seems that I think of it less and less these days, which is more than likely good...although I like thinking about it. It's not morbid at all, but rather uplifting. Makes me appreciate the days all the more. Makes you hold on tighter and love a little harder and sing a little louder. I am going to die and I am not going to push that too far back into my head. Too easy to take things for granted.

I am happier now than I have ever been in my life and I don't even know what that means. I like getting older. I like the lines on my face. I like the easiness I feel. I think about Gram out there and that makes me feel confident somehow. There is so much going on that we cannot see, or fail to see. So much to know that we will never know. It would be like going into a library and trying to figure out how to read every book. I would rather read one whole book than just skim through a thousand. Just the one, all the way through, is good enough for me...kind of like this life of ours.

jann

Nothing But Glamour
January 25, 2004

Hometown shows are hard on the heart. There were so many people I knew out there in the Calgary crowd. It's daunting and quite frankly, scares the living shit out of me. Very surreal indeed. It's like running through high school nude.

It is cold here in Saskatoon. Good Christ, what happened over night? I have my period to boot and it is so fun being on the bus, I cannot tell you. Nothing can go into the toilet, so I spend 4 rolls of toilet paper wrapping everything up so no one is the wiser. Oh the glamour is at its highest on the first day of riding the blood boat on the God forsaken bus. People are always so enamoured with tour buses and they couldn't be more boring or more uncomfortable. We play a lot of Scrabble and we are now onto another game called "Shut the Box," a great dice game that they played on the old wooden ships 200 years ago. Really fun, simple but challenging.

We spend too much time wishing life away, "if I were like this, or if I were like that..." Pointless and self-defeating. You really have to train that voice in your head; you have to control it and fight with it and put it in its place. It can get so big that it drowns out the birds singing eventually. We are indeed our own worst enemies. We set out to destroy ourselves every day and wonder why we get sad. I haven't had time to be mean to myself on this trip.

I slept til 3 o'clock today. I needed it I guess. We were on the bus all night, got here at noon and then I went to the hotel to get a few more hours rest. If I don't sleep, I cannot sing. It's the one and only thing I need to do for myself, sleep. I don't have a warm-up routine, nothing...I just need to sleep. Anyhow, all is well. I could sleep again right now, but I've got to put the war paint on. I hate doing it...the makeup that

is...but I love it too.   I have enough makeup to build a house
out of it.   Must go...

ja

Minus Freaking Fifty-two
January 29, 2004

I am in the catering room in Thunder Bay. It isn't as cold here as it was in Winnipeg. It was a God awful 52 degrees below zero last night as we loaded the truck out...as "we" loaded the truck out, that's funny. I was in my dressing room eating watermelon and having a snort of wine as I watched those brave souls drag those boxes out through the mist and the snow and the freezing night air.

I haven't heard what my dad's blood pressure is...no news is good news.

We drove last night on the bus...no really we were in a Lear jet...no actually the army took us all in tanks. I haven't slept. Grabbed a couple of hours this morning at the hotel, thank the Lord, so I'll get through it all right tonight. If I don't sleep, I don't sing very well...I sound like I am under a blanket with a rowdy midget. Boy that sounds odd. I better go lie down before I fall asleep.

j

In Other News
February 9, 2004

The world is a strange and wondrous place. I made the mistake of turning on the news today. The earth, it seems, is in continuous peril because of human stupidity; all the fighting, all the misery, all the wasted souls that battle for this mysterious tower of power. The battle for the domination of all things rages in the hearts of men. It's like *The Lord of the Rings,* only we don't have any good guys snuffing out evil along the way. We are getting to be fewer...

It seems so weird to me. I cannot understand the reasons and I doubt very much the people running around with the bombs and the guns and the hatred hanging off of their sleeves can either. They fight because they know that they are mortal and they don't want to die without taking somebody else with them...just a theory. It breaks me; the whole mess tears at something inside me that I cannot quite articulate. It's a light that gets dimmer and dimmer as I get older. I know I can only change what is within me, but when that essence is at battle with a force bigger than everything, it gets increasingly hard. I just go to sleep and hope that the earth will be there in the morning.

In other headlines...and here's where it's so bloody crazy...Brit Spears caught watching porn in her hotel room... Jesus...who hasn't done that??? Poor kid. I am going to miss the Grammy's tonight as I am working (I love seeing the fashion victims parading around). Maybe somebody will whip their dink out. That would be a refreshing change from tits.

In other news...the tour...the shows are going really well. The band is really playing great. I am proud of them. We laugh as much as we can and try as hard as our hearts will allow, taking people with us on our way. My nerves every night take longer and longer to wrangle under control. I can hardly breathe for the first two songs. It never ceases to amaze me that after all these years I still feel somewhat sick to my pants. I can see my heart beating through my clothes. My teeth rattle and my feet feel numb, other than that, it's really fun.

I haven't talked to my parents for 4 or 5 days. They sold their house. It's so sad. I feel so lost about it, conflicted. Change is a strange thing. It eats away at you like a bird tugging at a worm in the ground. But it's the newness that keeps us going; it's what we are, changelings. We have to be or we'd perish forever.

Maury just gave Russ $10 bucks to eat cheesecake with hot sauce on it...rock and roll is alive and well.

jann

I'd Go To Newfoundland
February 19, 2004

If there were ever a war raging over my head, I mean right over my head, in my backyard, I'd hop on a plane to Newfoundland. I'd pack up my cats, a few of my favourite books, my parents and their dog, a couple of cans of Clamato juice and I'd fly into St. John's and set up shop in one of the turquoise houses on the hillside overlooking the harbour. I'd buy a boat and a crab trap and a good pair of rubber boots and a pocketknife. I'd unplug the phone and throw the television into the abyss and sit on a wooden kitchen chair and learn to play the fiddle.

I'd go for long walks and talk to everybody that passed me by. I'd start with a "How do you do?" and finish up with a "See ya later on tonight then at Trader John's will I?" And they would say, "Well that'll be fine, Trader John's it is then." I'd whistle all day long, made up songs that had no beginning and no end in sight. I'd stand on the edge of the world and watch the black Atlantic swallow the sky. I'd catch the wind in my mouth and hold it deep inside my lungs until I couldn't anymore. I'd lick the salt from the backs of my hands and shout poetry across the waves. I'd work in a tiny café that served breakfast all day long, no questions asked, and I'd pour hot coffee as long as the poor souls could throw it back. I'd learn to bake bread and make soda buns and drink rum. I'd have a good laugh at the top of every hour.

I'd walk up hill all the time and never complain, because war would never find me in Newfoundland. The bombs would simply forget about us because we were no trouble to anybody. The clouds would hide us all from them. The ocean would be our giant moat where no dragon would ever dare cross. War wouldn't be bothered with we merry few. I would go to Newfoundland if they ever came to get us. I'd take my dear heart friends and my 3rd grade teacher, Mrs. Macrae, and I'd open a bed and breakfast and drink tea well into the afternoon if the guns ever came ablaring. I'd bring my Carpenters records and my favourite jeans and 4 pairs of wool socks and I'd walk around town looking at the little cemeteries and the blue and red doors with the Christmas wreaths still hanging proudly on them.

I would never be afraid coming home at 3 in the morning; I'd be fine. I'd get a yellow rain hat and sit and feed the gulls bits of the bread that I had learned to make. I'd make friends with old ladies and talk to them about how silly the war is anyhow and stuff like that. I'd sing just because it was quiet and I could hear the song for a change. I wouldn't HAVE to, I'd want to. I would like myself a little bit better every day,

because people would be so very nice to me and mean it. I'd wave at the whales and the fish and the boats and the stars. I'd pray out loud and not care what anybody thought because they'd be praying out loud too. I'd wish more. I'd hope for everybody to do well. I wouldn't care how many records I sold. I would never lie again in Newfoundland. I wouldn't be afraid to cry just because I felt happy. I would never exercise, I would just walk and keep breathing in and out and that would be amply good. I wouldn't care what day it was or what time it was; just knowing it was night or day would be fine by me.

God comes to Newfoundland when he needs a break from all the badness in the world. He comes for a beer and a solid shoulder to lean on. He doesn't even mind the PST.

I am tired and heading home.

j

Candles, Silence And Thunks

February 22, 2004

My parents are packing up their lives. The dog is the only one lying there without an inkling of the things to come. I went over a few hours ago to borrow some brown sugar, as I am attempting to make banana bread. It looks as though it turned out. I don't know, as I have not sawed the thing open yet; could be a brick actually.

The sun is shards of loveliness pouring down on the hills. I shall watch it slip over the horizon here, from the comfort of my flowered couch. The fire is on. I am dreaming strange

things, none of which make enough sense to even write down, so I won't. I have let Shrodie in and out at least a dozen times. He is going to run me into the nuthouse. I sometimes think he speaks to me. I swear to God he can say "no." Other than these exciting things, life is quiet.

The contrast of where I was last week to now, sitting here with candles and silence and thoughts being thunk... I never have time to think when I am on the road. It is simply too fast and too much out there, in that land so seemingly unreal. I stand in front of all those beautiful faces and look upon them with such awe, although I doubt they know. I try and tell them, but I fumble over heavy words. They fall flat somehow onto the stage floor. I am so thankful.

I am going to be old and none of this will matter but for a moment. I will be dealing with God and living and dying. All of this will be a faded memory of things that were never important. What we think is important, seldom is. We don't know what we are doing. I wish I could have some clue at some point.

That's all for now.

ja